Merrily Ever After

Book 3

A Novel By
D. Thrush

Cover design by Bukovero
Title page art courtesy of Clipart
Drawings by D. Thrush

ASIN: B01MYZVRSY
ISBN-10: 1541096975
ISBN-13: 978-1541096974

Praise for *Merrily Ever After!*

"Third in the series and I'm addicted to them. Finished the first 3 in 3 days! Will hate to see this series end. Ok, on to #4!" JV

"Another great book in the Santina Series... touching, clever... These are characters that feel as real as people we know, as familiar as the North Pole is magical..." constant reader

"...feel good read, based on the wonderful premise that Santa and the fairy tale of Christmas are real..." David Lindsay

"...a fun read... Hopefully there will be a book 4..." David Reese

"Best of the three novels in the Santina Series... but you don't have to read the others to enjoy this one as Ms. Thrush is such a great writer... And, as always, the novel has great messages that underlie the plot." JV

"This series, about the first female Santa, just keeps getting better!" Linda

"...This series was an amazing series. I read these just before Christmas and I felt like a kid again." Connie

"...Kudos to the author!! Full five star rating!" Michael Heidle

Novels by D. Thrush

Chick Lit / Rom Com

The Santa Secret (Prequel)
The Daughter Claus (Book 1)
The Claus Cause (Book 2)
Merrily Ever After (Book 3)
The More the Merrier (Book 4)

Fairy Tale Karma

~*~*~*~*~*~*~*~*~*~*~*~

Literary & Women's Fiction

Guardian of the Light

Whims & Vices (Book 1)
Fate & Flirtations (Book 2)

All the Little Secrets (Book 1)
Little Secrets Revealed (Book 2)

~*~*~*~*~*~*~*~*~*~*~*~

Contents

1 *Wrong Number*

Santina Claus gazed out the window of the plane at the vast white landscape of clouds. She put her hand on her stomach to still the butterflies that fluttered erratically at the thought of meeting her boyfriend, George's family for the first time. The only time she'd been to Boston was to deliver presents on Christmas Eve. Since she'd taken over her father's job two seasons ago after his heart attack scare, she'd flown all over the world in the red sleigh on that one special night. She still couldn't believe that she was the new Santa and that the family history had revealed that the original Santa was supposed to be a woman all along. The synchronicity was staggering.

The past season had presented many challenges, but she'd persevered. Her father had initially been resistant to the improvements she'd made and his younger brother, Kris Kringle, had attempted to take over, but she'd weathered all the turmoil. Everything had fallen into place and now she was looking forward to a nice, relaxing vacation with George before the new season began.

She reached into her carry-on for her Kindle, though she knew she wouldn't be able to concentrate on reading just yet. She was too wound up with warm memories of New Year's Eve a week ago. She saw her phone in her bag and wondered again who had called her repeatedly during the last few days. She didn't recognize the caller ID, and they'd left no message. It was probably just a sales call. Next time her phone rang, she'd answer it and ask them to quit calling.

Her thoughts returned to her recent reunion with George. Her parents had picked her up at the airport after her long flight from the North Pole. She was wiped out from all the deliveries on Christmas Eve. It was a magical night, but took a lot out of her. Her father understood better than anyone, and she slept on and off all the next day.

Her brother, Nicholas Junior's band *Black Ice,* was playing at their usual New Year's Eve gig. George was the lead guitar player, and she'd shown up early to greet the guys before they began their set. They were still arranging their equipment on the small stage when she spotted her brother with his spiky white hair and black eyeliner. Her hair was the same striking white color as their parents'.

"Now Tina, don't stay out too late," her mother, Clara, had admonished. "You're still recuperating."

Nick spotted her and jumped off the stage. "Hey, Tina." He gave her a hug. "You look tired. How did it go?"

"The delivery went well." She stifled a yawn.

Their father had attempted to groom Nick to inherit the role of Santa, but he'd turned down the honor, hoping to become a rock star. Despite everything resolving nicely, it still saddened her that he rejected their entire family legacy. Some of his songs slammed everything that the Claus family stood for.

"Right." Nick nodded. "I'm glad you're here. I've got a bunch of new songs, 'Snow Doom,' 'Naughtier Than Nice'…"

"Nick." Tina groaned in exasperation.

"And the one I wrote for Isabella called 'Rock Me.' She might be here tonight, and then we'll do the one we wrote together called 'Frozen Dreams.'" He scanned the room anxiously.

Nick had a major crush on Isabella, who was the lead singer of the hot all-female band *Rock Goddess.* He'd met her when *Black Ice* had opened for them on tour. He tried to be cool about it while she remained tantalizingly elusive. Loren, another guitarist, flirted with her outrageously in front of him. Tina wasn't sure if he did it to annoy Nick or he was genuinely interested in her too. Such a soap opera. But Isabella was a no-show that night and Nick was despondent.

"Tina." George swept her up into an embrace. "I missed you," he said in her ear.

"I missed you too. I wish we had more time together."

"I know. I have to fly out the day after tomorrow, but we'll have lots of time together in Boston," he promised.

And now here she was, staring at the clouds out the window of the plane and sighing as she remembered the songs he'd sung from the stage that night. He called her his muse, and his lyrics conveyed how he felt about her. It was so romantic.

"This year is going to be great," George said after they'd kissed at midnight. And she believed him.

Tina had spent some time in Florida with her parents and brother before she'd gotten back on a plane. She'd needed the time to recuperate, and it was relaxing to soak up the sun on the beach after the frenzy of the end of the season. She could understand why this job had aged her father and was glad to see he'd lost weight and looked healthier. He was clean-shaven and wore a baseball hat whenever they went anywhere. Her mother told her that no one had recognized him in some time.

She wondered if the word would get out that there was a new Santa. She hoped not. It was funny that her brother sought fame and recognition as a rock star while she craved anonymity. It was ironic because they'd experienced the downside of celebrity growing up. Everyone knew who they were at the North Pole, and they were never sure if kids were their friends because of their father.

Tina knew Lisa was a true friend. They'd become friends in Florida while Tina was attending college before Lisa had learned who she was. Lisa had eventually tricked Nick into telling her, and now she was Tina's indispensable assistant at the North Pole.

She gave up on the idea of reading and tucked her

Kindle back into her carry-on. Settling back in her seat and turning toward the window, she let her thoughts wander. Gliding through the clouds, with the brisk wind rushing by, the thickness of the reins, the bumpiness of their hasty landings on each roof. Had they forgotten the presents? Before she knew it, she was jostled awake by turbulence. Butterflies resumed their mad dance when she remembered she would soon see George again.

She'd felt drawn to him from the moment she'd first seen him in her brother's band, and he'd felt the same way. But she'd worried when the band had gone out on tour. She was afraid he'd forget all about her. But he hadn't. In fact, Lisa had arranged for him to surprise her at the North Pole and he'd kissed her for the first time at the Northern Lights Festival under the mistletoe. And now they were dealing with a long-distance relationship as their jobs took them in different directions. They'd vowed to make it work. Somehow.

George was waiting for her at the baggage claim, and she rushed into his arms. They squeezed each other tightly. She never wanted to let go.

"Welcome to Boston," he said. "My parents' house is on the outskirts, and it's not too far. I feel bad taking you away from the sun and back to snow."

"I don't care where we are," Tina replied. "As long as we're together."

His dark hair was pulled back into a ponytail and he wore a green skullcap and black ski jacket. He grabbed her flowered suitcase off the baggage carousel and she unzipped it to retrieve her purple jacket for the colder weather.

"The car has a good heater," he said, rolling her suitcase behind him.

She trailed behind him through the swarm of travelers. "I'm a little nervous about meeting your family," she admitted when they got to the car.

"You don't have to be nervous. They'll love you."

They quickly got into the car and George started it. "You're going to meet my older brother and younger sister and my grandmother. Since my grandfather died last year, she's been living with my parents."

Tina remembered when that had happened right before the band was about to go on tour and she was due to return to the North Pole to begin the season. It had cut short their time together and disrupted the beginning of the tour, but George had returned home in time to bid his grandfather goodbye before he'd slipped away.

Tina tried to subdue her butterflies while they drove through the snowy streets. Drifts spilled over the curbs and people hurried along the sidewalks, bundled up. The day was gray, with evening quickly stealing the light. Her stomach growled, and she realized she hadn't eaten much that day. It soothed her a bit when George took her hand.

He pulled into the driveway of a two-story house. Snow draped the roof and smoke curled up from the chimney. They retrieved the suitcase from the trunk and she timidly followed him up the path and inside.

A Christmas tree twinkling with lights stood in the living room and an enticing aroma reminded Tina that she was hungry. George hung up their coats in the closet.

"Oh, you're here!" An older woman with dark shoulder-length hair appeared. "You must be Tina. I'm so happy to meet you." She grabbed Tina into a hug.

"This is my mother, Gloria." George laughed.

"Nice to meet you," Tina said when Gloria released her.

"Come in. We'll worry about your suitcase later." Gloria waved her hand and led her into the living room.

There were several people watching TV while a fire crackled in the fireplace. Family photos hung on the walls, and Christmas decorations adorned the room.

"I know it's past Christmas, but I just love the

holidays. I don't take the tree down until I have to," Gloria said. "Grover, this is George's friend, Tina. This is George's father."

Grover stood up. "Come on in and have a seat. I'm just watching the game."

"Thank you," Tina said as George led her over to the L-shaped couch.

"Grandma, this is my girlfriend, Tina."

The older woman had gray hair and wore glasses. She wore a sweatshirt adorned with a Christmas tree and a fleece blanket covered her knees. Tina noticed her purple fuzzy slippers.

"Nice to meet you." She smiled kindly.

Tina returned her smile. She hoped she could remember everyone's names.

"We call her G.G. for Grandma Grace," George said. "Is Garrett here, Mom?"

"He's in the kitchen making his pecan pie."

"He makes the best pecan pie," George told Tina.

"Talking about me already?"

A young man came out of the kitchen. He resembled George except that his hair was shorter and he had a beard and mustache. He extended his hand.

"This is my brother, Garrett," George said as Garrett shook her hand. "My parents like G names."

"Yeah, I'm lucky I wasn't Grover Junior," Garrett remarked.

"There's nothing wrong with that name," their father said.

"Dad, you know they have a Muppet from *Sesame Street* with that name, right?" Garrett shook his head. "I would've been teased so badly in school."

"Tina, are you hungry? Dinner is almost finished," Gloria said. "George didn't tell me if you're a vegetarian like he is. There's plenty either way."

"Uh, not really." She glanced at George. She tried to be sensitive to his food choices and ate as he did when they were together. "But my parents have eaten that way since my father's heart attack."

"Oh, dear. I hope he's okay," G.G. commented.

"Yes, he's completely recovered and a lot healthier now," Tina assured her.

"George told us you've been managing your family's business since your father got sick." Grover pulled his attention from the TV. "I think he said it's a toy company."

That vague description always made Tina smile. "Yes. That's right. My father retired and I'm going to continue running the company."

"Is it a company we would've heard of?" Garrett asked.

"No. I don't think so." Tina shook her head.

"It's a huge international company, but not a well-known brand," George explained. "Tina's done a great job and made a lot of improvements."

Tina shrugged. "I enjoy it." She didn't like talking about it because it led to too many questions. "What do you do, Garrett?"

"Me? I'm a chef. Hence the baking." He grinned. "Mom, we should probably round everybody up to eat."

***

After dinner, George lugged Tina's suitcase upstairs to his sister's old room. It had a full-size bed covered with a quilt. There was also a desk, bookshelves, and a small TV.

"It's too bad your sister is sick and I couldn't meet her yet," Tina said, admiring the cozy room.

"I'm sure she'll be around when she feels better," George said. "Everyone has been curious about you."

"Oh, she has a window seat." Tina noticed with delight.

"Yeah, she used to sit there and read for hours."

"What does she do?" Tina sat on the cushioned seat.

"She's a writer." He sat beside her. "Garrett's wife is

a teacher and they have a son who's four. I think she's out of town visiting her family, but Garrett said you'll get a chance to meet them tomorrow."

"You didn't tell me you have a little nephew. I love kids."

"I hope so. You're San..."

"Don't say it!" Tina put her hand over his mouth, and they both laughed. "Your mother sure likes to decorate for the holidays."

"She loves Christmas. She'd freak if she knew who you really were."

Tina's phone rang, and she got up to fetch it from her carry-on. Sure enough, it was the same unrecognizable caller ID.

"I keep getting these sales calls. I'm going to tell them to quit calling me," she said to George. "Hello?"

"Is this Santina Claus?" a female voice asked.

Tina was stunned for a moment. "Who is this?" she demanded. How would anybody know her real name and phone number? "I'm sorry. I'm not interested in whatever you're selling. Please don't call me again."

"I'm not selling anything," the woman said quickly. "My name is Jill Graham, and I work for *Modern Woman's World* magazine. I'd like to interview you."

"Interview me? I think you have the wrong number," Tina protested. "I don't want a subscription to the magazine."

"Is this Santina Claus?" Jill asked again. "Just hear me out for a minute. The world has a right to know who you are..."

"I'm sorry. You have the wrong number." Tina hung up the phone in a panic. She looked at George with wide eyes.

"What happened? Who was that?" George asked with concern.

"It was a reporter. She wants to interview me. She knows who I am," Tina blurted. "What am I going to do? My father is going to be furious. He doesn't want anyone to know who we are outside of the North Pole."

"Don't worry. It's not your fault." George rubbed her arm. "How would this person know about you or how to find you?"

"That's the question." Tina furrowed her brow. "Someone had to tip her off."

But who could it be?

2 *Family Feud*

"Hi, Mom," Tina said into the phone while she paced in the bedroom.

"Tina! Dear, Tina's on the phone... I don't know yet. I just got on the phone with her..."

"Mom," Tina called her attention back to their conversation.

"Yes, I'm here. How's your visit going? How is George's family? I'm sure they're as wonderful as he is."

Clara liked him. They often exchanged vegetarian recipes.

"Yes, they're very nice. We're going out to brunch at the restaurant where his brother works in a little while. He's a chef. Everyone is great. I'm still pretty tired, though."

"It can take weeks to recover your energy. Sometimes it took your father a month before he felt back to normal," Clara said. "Your brother and your cousin, Kris, are coming over for dinner tonight."

"Oh? How are they?"

"I spoke to Nick on the phone and he was complaining about his guitar player. He doesn't sound very happy with him."

"That's only because Nick and Loren both like Isabella."

"Is she the singer from the band they toured with? What were they called? Stone something..."

"Yes, she's the singer for *Rock Goddess*. They both like her," Tina said with exasperation.

Why were they talking about Nick's problems?

"I'm glad that Kris is working as a roadie for Nick now," Clara went on. "I think he's much happier working with the band than he would've been as Santa at the North Pole. Otherwise, we could've had an ugly fight on our hands. Can you imagine if that would've ended up in court? So much for being anonymous."

"Yes, I'm glad it worked out. I don't think Uncle Kris

would've taken it to court anyway. Would he?"

"I suppose you're right. Probably not."

Tina recalled when her father's brother, Kris Kringle, sent his incompetent son, Kris Junior, to the North Pole to take it over from her, arguing that Santa had never been a woman. Little did they know about the true family history at the time. But Tina had stood her ground, trusting that she was the best person for the job. It had been a tough year for her.

"Mom, the reason I called is..."

"Hang on. Your father wants to say hello," Clara interrupted.

"Tina," her father said gruffly. "Have you talked to Walter? I want to make sure that he shuts off the auxiliary power and not the main power. Things can freeze if the main power is shut off."

"Dad, why didn't you mention this last week? Walter is on vacation with Lisa now. Besides, I'm sure he knows which power source to shut off before he leaves. He does it every year."

"Well, I'm going to come up this year and see how you're doing. I heard good things from my brother. He said you knew how to handle the sleigh, but I can give you a few pointers. I'm sure you're doing a fine job, but I never had the chance to explain a few things to you."

"Uh, okay. You and Mom are welcome to come up any time. I'd love for you to see the improvements I've made and..."

"Here's your mother," he said abruptly.

"Just a minute, Tina," Clara said. "I'm taking the phone into the bedroom so your father can watch TV. Okay, here we are. Let me just shut the door. Okay. You know your father just wants to feel useful again. I don't think it makes him feel good to hear how great things are going without him."

"Oh, sorry. I didn't think of that. I just want him to know that I'm doing a good job, and he doesn't have to worry about the business," Tina said defensively.

"Yes, I understand, but try to be a little more sensitive to his feelings. Now I should go. I have to start dinner."

"But it's only morning."

"I know. I have to throw everything into the crockpot, so I'd better get chopping. Last time, the carrots weren't quite cooked. Goodness, your father is calling me. I never get a moment."

"Mom, don't hang up. I have to ask you something," Tina said. "It can't wait."

"What is it? Is everything okay? Don't scare me."

"I just wanted to ask you if anyone ever discovered who dad was. I mean, did he ever do any interviews or anything like that?"

"Goodness, no. We were very careful. Now I know George knows who we are, but I don't want you to tell his family, if that's what you're asking."

"I won't."

"Good. I'd better get going. Have fun visiting George's family."

"I will."

Tina sat on the window seat overlooking the snow-covered patio in the backyard. Maybe the reporter would get discouraged and stop calling her. After all, she couldn't do an interview without the interviewee, could she? She decided not to let it ruin her vacation with George. She'd looked forward to this time with him for too long and didn't want anything to mar it. She might be worrying for nothing.

***

Tina sat at the large oval table with George's family. The restaurant was beautiful, with stained-glass windows, crisp white tablecloths, and a festive wreath centerpiece. Garrett's wife, Tonia, and their four-year-old son, Evan, had joined them. He was a cute little boy with dark curly hair and dark eyes. Tina wondered what she'd delivered to him at Christmas. She wasn't as good at remembering as her father was yet. Perhaps this was a skill that would develop over time. Garrett prepared their meals and stopped by their table to see how they were enjoying their food. They sipped champagne from crystal goblets while conversation flowed.

"Do you do this every weekend?" Tina wondered. The champagne gave her a warm, relaxed feeling.

Gloria let out a hearty laugh. "I wish."

"This is because you're here," George told her. "Everyone is happy to meet you."

"Oh." Tina felt herself blushing.

"You must be very busy during the holidays," Tonia stated. She had short dark hair and kind eyes.

"What do you mean?" Tina asked.

"You know, selling toys at Christmas."

"Oh yes, we are." Tina looked at Evan, who was staring at her. "What did Santa bring you?"

"My friend says there's no Santa and Mommy and Daddy buy my presents," he responded solemnly.

Tonia sighed. "What can we say to that? We don't want to be untruthful with him."

"Oh, Evan," Tina cried. "There really is a Santa. I know there is."

She glanced around the table and tried to regain her composure. But it bothered her to hear a young child deny her existence.

"How do you know?" Evan asked, wide-eyed.

"I can tell that you know deep down that Santa is real, don't you?" Tina said. "I've seen the North Pole and the reindeer and the elves. It's important for you to believe in Santa because sh... Santa believes in you."

"Really?"

Tina could see he was torn between wanting to accept it and wanting to appear grown up as younger children tend to do. She hoped his parents wouldn't be upset that she was encouraging him, but she just had to. It broke her heart when children relinquished their belief in the magic of Christmas.

Tina looked at Tonia. "Children grow up too fast. I didn't mean to interfere, but I just..."

"No, it's fine," Tonia assured her. "You're probably more invested in the idea because of your family's toy company."

"Have you really seen the reindeer? Even Rudolph?" Evan asked with astonishment.

"Yes, I have," Tina answered with a smile. "There's Blitzen and Donner and Dasher and Dancer and Prancer and Vixen and Comet and Cupid and, of course, Rudolph. They're big and strong because they have to pull the sleigh filled with all the presents."

"I want to meet them too," Evan said earnestly.

"They like the cold, so they have to stay at the North Pole. Just remember to be good and write Santa a letter every year," Tina reminded him. "Sh... Santa loves to get letters."

"You have a good memory," Gloria observed. "I certainly couldn't remember the names of all the reindeer."

"I believe in Santa," George said with a grin. "In fact, I've met Santa."

"You never told me that," Evan accused.

"I know," George admitted. "Tina works at the toy shop and I got to see it. When I grew up, I thought I should stop believing in Santa, but I'm glad I believe again." He smiled at Tina.

"More pancakes." Garrett approached the table, carrying a tray. "Any more requests before I join you?"

"Come sit down with us," Tonia urged. "Tina's telling us about the North Pole."

"Oh." Tina waved her hand. "Just for Evan."

"Mommy, can I go to the North Pole and see the reindeer?" Evan asked.

"The reindeer go on vacation after Christmas," Tina said quickly.

"Maybe next year," Tonia answered.

Tina realized she should change the subject before she said too much and aroused suspicion.

"Does Garrett do all the cooking at home, Tonia? This is delicious."

***

"I probably shouldn't have said all that," Tina said to George as they dawdled behind everyone walking back to the cars. "I just couldn't stand to think of little Evan not believing."

"Don't worry. No one thought anything of it," he assured her.

"But he's not my kid and I should've let your brother and sister-in-law handle it," Tina fretted. "It's not my place..."

"It's your place more than anyone else with that subject," George answered with a smile.

"Yes, but they don't know that."

"I want to sit next to Tina," Evan wailed as they piled into the car.

"Evan, you have to come with me in our car," Tonia insisted firmly.

"But I want to sit next to Tina!"

"We can ride with you instead of Mom and Dad," George offered. "Kids like Tina."

"He usually wants to sit by me," Gloria said with surprise.

"I'm sorry." Tina felt bad.

"No, it's okay. You're the new person and he likes you. I'm glad. Go with Tonia." Gloria shooed them.

"I feel like I'm causing trouble," Tina confided to George.

"Yeah, you're a real troublemaker," he teased. He gave her a quick kiss. "Let's take a drive later and I can show you around town."

"Yes, I'd like to see where you hung out and went to school," Tina said. "You got to see where I grew up."

"You win. I can't beat that."

"I used to wish my family was just a regular family." Tina sighed. "But I can't complain."

Tonia strapped Evan into his booster seat in the back seat.

"I'll sit in the back with Evan," Tina told George. "Why don't you sit up front with Tonia?"

"Does Santa have any kids?" Evan asked as she put on her seatbelt.

"I think he has a boy and a girl," she answered hesitantly.

"What are their names?"

"I'm not sure." Tina changed the subject. "Are you going to school yet?"

"I go to preschool," he answered proudly.

***

"Come in, boys." Clara opened the door of the condo. "Hi, Nick. Kris, it's good to see you." She gave each of them a hug.

"Hey, Aunt Clara," Kris responded and shuffled over to the couch.

"Hey, Mom. Hey, Dad." Nick greeted them. "It smells good in here. I'm hungry."

Santa looked up from his recliner chair. "Kris, how are your parents?"

"You look funny without your beard and mustache," Kris commented.

Santa rubbed his scratchy chin. "I forgot to shave today. It looks like you forgot, too."

Kris touched the white goatee that matched his tousled hair. "No, this is on purpose."

Santa shook his head. "I don't get you kids today. This one wears makeup." He stuck his thumb in Nick's direction.

"Dad." Nick shook his head. "I'm an artist. I wear makeup on stage. It's a show." He plopped onto the couch with Kris.

"*Black Ice* puts on the best show I've ever seen," Kris enthused.

"It's too loud," Santa grumbled.

"It's supposed to be loud," Nick asserted. "I want to blast people out of their inertia."

"You're going to blast them out of their seats and on their way home," Santa responded. "If you don't break their eardrums first."

"Well, you certainly have a lot of fans," Clara interjected. "I'm glad you're enjoying your job with the band, Kris."

"I could've run the North Pole," he bragged. "How hard can it be if a girl can do it? Right?" He poked Nick.

"Huh?" Nick looked up from his phone.

"Tina does a fine job," Santa said.

"Now, Kris," Clara admonished. "Girls can do just about anything boys can do. I don't want to hear that kind of talk."

Kris let out a sarcastic laugh. "Yeah? Well, what about... sports? Huh? And what about... mailmen?"

Clara sighed. "There are mail women too and there are many successful female athletes."

"Nick, get off your phone," Santa ordered. "Your mother is talking."

"Huh?" Nick looked up. "Oh, Kris is doing great. When we're not on tour, he does other stuff for us."

"Yeah, I go get Nick's coffee every day," Kris said. "Tall mocha with whipped cream."

"Not every day," Nick said. "Sometimes I order..."

"Nick," Clara said sharply. "I hope you're not making Kris run around and do all your errands for you."

"Mom, that's what an assistant does," Nick protested.

Kris nodded enthusiastically. "I get to go to rehearsals and I help set up the microphones. If Nick's doing a new song, I turn the pages in his notebook so that he can sing the lyrics."

"Oh, for goodness sake." Clara threw up her hands. "You can't turn your own pages?"

"Mom, you don't understand," Nick groaned. "I'm into the emotion of the song. It breaks my concentration if I have to stop and turn the pages."

"Nick, don't you take advantage of your cousin," she scolded.

"My job is very important," Kris stated. "I'm part of the support team for the band. I get to do a lot of stuff the other guys don't get to do. Nick even gave me extra T-shirts. See?" He stuck his chest out so they could view his *Black Ice* shirt.

"Hmm." Clara looked at Santa.

"Well, the kid's happy, so what harm is there?" Santa asked. "Can you imagine him trying to run the business?" He chuckled.

"I could have done it if I wanted," Kris maintained.

"Yes, of course," Clara said. "We're just thinking about how different things would be, but everything worked out. Why don't we eat?"

Santa, Nick, and Kris got up and seated themselves at the dining room table. Clara had placed a basket of rolls in the center and they each grabbed one.

"Now don't everybody help me at once." Clara stood with her hands on her hips.

"Nick, help your mother," Santa demanded.

Clara frowned at him. "You too, dear."

"How much help do you need?" Santa grumbled as they followed her into the kitchen.

Clara ladled the stew from the crockpot into bowls.

"Now carry these out to the table. I'll bring the silverware."

"Where's the meat?" Kris asked, peering into his bowl.

"I told you my parents are vegetarians like George," Nick said.

"I know, but where's the meat?" he asked again.

"Vegetarians don't eat meat," Clara explained.

"I'm not a vegetarian," Santa objected.

"Fine, dear."

"What's in this?" Kris asked suspiciously, stirring it with his spoon.

"Potatoes, carrots, green beans, lentils, garlic, all kinds of healthy things," Clara answered.

"It's good, Mom," Nick said.

"Thank you, Nick." Clara took a bite. "Yum. Not too many rolls, dear," she said to Santa. "Oh, I talked to Tina today."

"Nick, put your phone away," Santa ordered.

"I have to answer a text."

"You have to eat this delicious meal your mother prepared and take part in this conversation." He pounded his fist on the table.

"Dear..." Clara put her hand on his arm. "Calm down."

"Your face gets red just like my father's, Uncle Nick," Kris noted.

"You have to watch your stress, Dad," Nick said. "I never get stressed."

"Because you're clueless," Santa muttered.

"I just get a little tense before I go onstage, but it psyches me up. It's a total adrenaline high, man."

"He rocks." Kris nodded.

"It's wonderful that you enjoy what you're doing," Clara said, dunking her roll in her bowl.

"I have to get my message out to the masses. People need to wake up to the brainwashing. What I do is important," Nick declared.

"What we do at the North Pole is important," Santa countered. "It's too bad you couldn't appreciate that when..."

"Now, now," Clara said patiently. "It all worked out. It's not Nick's thing. Tina was the best person for the job, after all."

"Except she's a girl," Kris said.

"Toys are trivial compared to the problems we have today," Nick intoned. "We need to be aware and rise up against the corporatocracy that's taken over. It's time for revolution."

"Trivial?" Santa bellowed.

"Revolution?" Clara furrowed her brow. "Okay. Enough of this talk at the table. You're upsetting your father."

"The family business isn't trivial," Santa said adamantly.

"Of course not, dear," she assured him. "Everyone, eat your stew before it gets cold."

"Dad, I don't think you get what I do. My songs wake people up..."

"You need to wake up to reality," Santa responded. "The family business is not trivial. I dedicated my entire adult life to the mission of delivering toys all over the world..."

"Toys are trivial, Dad."

"Nick, please stop saying that," Clara implored. "Our business brings joy to all the children..."

"Uncle Nick, your face is getting red again," Kris noticed.

"And Kris." Clara turned to him. "I don't want to hear another word about Tina being a girl."

"But she is a girl, Aunt Clara."

"I know she's a girl, I mean woman, but she's just as capable..."

"She's capable of being a corporate cog, but that's her thing." Nick shrugged.

"Cog." Kris snickered.

"Listen to me, Nick." Santa pointed his finger at him. "I will not have you diminish my life's work or that of your sister. I don't know where we went wrong with you that you don't respect the legacy of this family."

"I agree with Nick," Kris piped up. "The other guys think he's too political, but not me."

"And you just shut up!" Santa pointed at him.

"Dad, quit freaking out." Nick frowned.

"I am not freaking out!"

"That's enough!" Clara cried. "Please eat your stew!" She took a deep breath. "What is wrong with this family? Can't we have one meal together without arguing? Geez Louise."

There was only the sound of chewing and slurping for a moment.

"I'm eating. See?" Santa lifted a spoonful to his mouth. "Mmm. Delicious."

3 *It Takes a Village*

"Walter, you were right. It really is beautiful here," Lisa said, staring out at the aqua blue ocean.

They were sitting in lounge chairs on the pristine beach, wearing straw hats and sunglasses. They each held a drink made with tropical fruit juices.

"The sand looks so white. Is it whiter than in Florida?"

"I think it is, but it also looks that way because the water is so blue," Walter answered. "This is just what I need at the end of the season. It melts away my stress so I can be ready to get back to work. That's why I like to come here every year."

"I don't know why I didn't want to come with you last year." Lisa frowned. "I guess I was confused about what I wanted."

Her flirtation with Loren, the new guitarist in Nick's band, had distracted her for sure.

"I was probably pressuring you too much," Walter admitted. "I know things moved pretty fast between us and we have a lot of differences to consider."

"Oh, you know that stuff doesn't matter to me," she assured him. "I don't care about our age difference or height difference." She sipped her drink. "Why? Does it bother you? Have you ever been involved with anyone who wasn't an elf?"

She'd never asked him that before, and now she was curious.

He set his drink down on the sand. "Not really. I haven't been in that many relationships. I was married for a long time and the divorce traumatized me. I never thought I'd want to be in another relationship."

"And then you met me." She smiled.

"Yes, Tina's crazy friend." He chuckled. "You were drunk the first time I met you at the North Pole when you came to visit Tina."

"I was?" She scrunched up her nose. "I don't

remember."

"I rest my case." He grinned. "And then you just never left."

"You're stuck with me now."

Walter looked over at Lisa. "I'm glad we worked everything out. You did the right thing when you showed up at my house that night and made me talk to you."

"I knew I didn't want to lose you, Walter."

"Good. Then we're stuck with each other."

Lisa thought back to the time last year when she'd felt torn between Loren and Walter. Loren was fun and easygoing. He'd flirted with her relentlessly in Florida when Walter had been upset at her indecisiveness about their relationship. Loren's attention had been flattering, and his kiss had made her dizzy. But she'd finally realized that he wasn't really interested in her, except in the moment, and she wanted more than that. That experience had made her appreciate Walter's loyalty and honesty and stability. Her feelings for him had deepened once she'd stopped denying them. She was glad she'd come to her senses. And now life was good.

"Have you heard from Tina since we've been here?" Walter's eyes were closed as he soaked in the sun's rays.

"We texted a few times. She was nervous about meeting George's family."

"I wonder how things are going."

"Oh, you know they'll love her. Who doesn't love Tina?" Lisa asked.

"That's true," Walter acknowledged.

***

Tina sat cross-legged by the fireplace. Evan spilled the wooden pieces from the tin container onto the carpet and they scattered all over. She laughed as she began to study the pamphlet.

"We can make an entire town of houses from all these."

"I want to make some cars, too," he informed her.

"Okay. And it looks like you've got some people for your town."

Evan was busily placing the interlocking wooden pieces together while Tina built the semblance of a house. George came out of the kitchen and came over.

"I see Evan has you helping him with his construction project," he noted with a smile.

Tina looked up at him. "We're going to build an entire town. Right, Evan?"

"And some cars," he reminded her.

"That sounds like a lot of work. I'd better help you." George sat down on the carpet beside Tina.

They constructed several houses and two cars while chatting with Evan, who placed the little people inside each structure.

"What a great village," G.G. said when she hobbled into the room. She'd had knee replacement surgery and was still recovering.

"Let me help you." Tina jumped up and took her hand as she eased onto the couch.

"Thank you, Tina. Have a seat next to me." G.G. patted the cushion beside her. "Evan really likes you."

"I love kids. They have such pure spirits."

Tina settled on the couch beside George's grandmother. A fire crackled in the fireplace and the Christmas tree lights twinkled, making her feel right at home.

"You know, George was such a good little boy. Garrett was always causing trouble, and Gemma would have tantrums if she didn't get her way. But not George. He was calm even as a kid."

"Do you have any pictures? I'd love to see them."

"Yes, we do. You've probably seen the ones on the walls, but there are a few photo albums around here somewhere. George, do you know where your mother keeps them?"

"You really want to see pictures of me as a little kid?" George scowled at Tina and shook his head.

"Of course! I bet you were so cute." She smiled at the thought.

"Okay. I'll get them. I think they're in the den." He got up.

"Come sit next to me, Evan," G.G. said. "We're going to look at pictures."

"Of me?" he asked.

"Of Uncle George when he was a little boy."

George returned, holding a thick photo album. "Be careful," he said as he set it on G.G.'s lap. "A lot of the pictures are loose, and they're falling out." He pulled an ottoman over to sit on.

G.G. opened the cover and turned the pages carefully. The photos were displayed under a layer of clear plastic. Some of them stayed in place, but many of them were loose. She gently turned the pages until she came upon some pictures of George.

"That's him." She pointed to a small dark-haired boy in a playpen.

"Aw, how cute," Tina cried. "It looks like your hair used to be curly like Evan's."

"He had beautiful curly hair when he was a child," G.G. confirmed.

George shrugged. "I don't remember."

Tina enjoyed perusing the family photos. She saw pictures of George's parents, Gloria and Grover, when they were younger, and many pictures of the three siblings. There were a few photos of George with his grandfather. This made G.G. a little sad.

"They were so close, you know," she said softly.

They heard the front door open and close, and Tina was glad for the distraction.

"Hey, everybody."

A young woman with long dark hair poked her head into the room. She removed her coat and hung it in the closet before she approached and bent down to give G.G. a hug.

"Hi, Grandma."

"Are you feeling better?" G.G. asked.

"Yeah. I'm still a little stuffed up, but a lot better," she answered. "Don't worry. I'm not contagious."

"Gemma, this is Tina," George said, rising to give her a hug. "Tina, this is my sister, Gemma."

"I've really been looking forward to meeting you," Gemma said.

"It's been nice meeting everyone." Tina stood.

Gemma stared at her. "You're really pretty. I've never seen white hair like that on a young person."

"Oh." Tina felt herself blushing. "I love your hair. It's so thick."

"Thanks, and welcome to Boston." She pulled Tina into an embrace. "Okay, I want to hear all about how you met, but leave out all the mushy stuff. Right, Evan? Don't I get a hug?"

Evan got off the couch and went over to give her a hug. She stooped down.

"Look at these cool houses. Did you build all that?"

"George and Tina helped me," he said. "I made the cars."

"I like the cars best." Gemma nodded. "George, I listened to the last CD. I really like your song 'Full Heart.' Did you write that one for Tina? It's beautiful."

"Yeah, thanks," George answered. "You should come see another show next time we go on tour. We always have new songs."

"That's a great idea."

"I've been staying in your old room. I love the window seat," Tina commented.

"Yeah. Isn't it great? I used to sit there and read all the time," Gemma responded. "Actually, I have to run up there for a minute. Come with me."

"Okay." Tina glanced at George and then followed Gemma up the stairs.

"I still have some stuff in here," Gemma said as they entered the room. She went straight to the window and sat on the padded seat. "I used to read for hours right here." She noticed Tina's phone beside her. "Is this your phone?"

"Yes." Tina crossed the room and picked it up. She'd missed some calls from the same number. That reporter was persistent. How annoying. She sat on the window seat and gazed out the window with Gemma.

"How did you meet my brother?" Gemma asked. "Not that he hasn't told us how captivated he was the first time he saw you."

"He did?" Tina hoped she wasn't blushing. "We met through my brother, Nick. They started *Black Ice* together. I guess we both had crushes on each other."

"I met Nick. He has the same white hair as you. I met the whole band when they played here in Boston," Gemma explained. "Nick's interesting. I wasn't sure what you'd be like after I met him."

Tina gave a little laugh. "That's one way to put it. We're very different in a lot of ways."

"No offense, but I'm glad." Gemma laughed, too.

"I've enjoyed meeting your family," Tina said. "Everyone is very nice."

"Well, we've all been looking forward to meeting *you*," Gemma said. "George doesn't get seriously involved that often."

Tina nodded while watching a bird hop around on the snow in the yard. A pedestal feeder stood a few feet away. Evergreen boughs were weighted with snow and smoke curled up from the chimney next door.

"So, what are your intentions?"

Tina looked at her serious expression with surprise. "Uh..."

Gemma burst out laughing. "I'm kidding, Tina."

***

"I love this skirt," Lisa said, touching the silky fabric on a hanger. "But when would I ever get a chance to wear it?"

"Whenever we're here or in Florida," Walter responded. "Buy it if you like it."

"Let's look around a little more. There's so much great stuff."

They strolled amongst the shopping stalls in the marketplace. Bright colors adorned the clothing and there were so many tempting choices, but Lisa knew she couldn't buy too much or she wouldn't be able to close her suitcase. She'd already purchased a cloth shopping bag and assorted trinkets, and Walter had bought her a beautiful necklace with a silver diamond-cut palm tree dangling from the chain. She touched it. She hadn't taken it off since he'd given it to her. It would be a constant reminder of this fabulous vacation.

Lisa was drawn to a table displaying handwoven baskets. She noticed some people pointing and turned to see that Walter was the object of their interest. She looked around to see that people were staring at him. She felt terrible that he had to endure this type of attention, but she couldn't blame them. How often do you see someone of his stature? He was a curiosity, yet he seemed unaware of their stares. He was probably used to it, though at the North Pole, he wasn't an oddity. How disconcerting to have to deal with this every time he left home.

Lisa went over and took his hand. He smiled at her and she felt great affection for him. He was the nicest person she knew, and she felt incredibly lucky. She heard the muffled sound of her phone and pulled it out of her bag. Maybe it was Tina. Nope. She didn't recognize the number on the caller ID.

"Hello?"

"Hi, is this Lisa?"

"Yeah, who's this?"

"Good. This is Jill Graham from *Modern Woman's*

World magazine..."

"That's a mouthful," Lisa said.

"Tell me about it," the woman answered. "Anyway, I'm a journalist for the magazine and I'm doing a story on Santina Claus. My sources tell me you're her assistant. I'd like to set up an interview..."

"What sources?" Lisa demanded, taken aback.

Tina would never agree to an interview. The Claus family was adamant about remaining anonymous. How could this journalist know about them? How would she know about her?

"I'm sorry. I can't reveal my sources. I can come to you wherever you are..."

"I'm on vacation," Lisa said.

"Okay. Then can you confirm that you work for Santina Claus?"

"Who? I don't know what you're talking about," Lisa said. "Sorry. I can't help you."

"I'll come to you or we can do this over the phone if you prefer..."

"Sorry." Lisa hung up her phone.

"Who was it?" Walter asked, noting her expression.

"Oh, my gosh, Walter! It was a journalist." Lisa realized people were looking their way. "Let's go."

They hurried down the street until they were away from the crowd. Lisa's heart was pounding from the brief conversation.

"What did she want?" Walter asked with apprehension.

"She wants to do a story on Tina and she wants to interview me, too. How does she know about us? Has this ever happened before?"

"I don't think so." He scratched his clean-shaven chin.

"She said she has sources," Lisa remembered. "Who could they be? None of us would go to a journalist."

"I don't know." He shook his head, befuddled.

"Walter, what should we do?" she fretted.

"You have to tell Tina. You have to warn her," he said decisively.

"You're right. I'll text her." She stared at her phone. "What am I going to say? I don't want to freak her out while she's visiting George." She considered this for a moment. "But I have to warn her."

"A journalist contacted me. She knows who you are. Don't worry. I didn't say anything. Just giving you a heads up. Say hi to George." She pressed Send.

"Maybe I should've called, but she won't be able to talk in front of George's family."

"If this woman found you, she probably already contacted Tina," Walter deduced. "Who would talk to the press, though?"

"You don't think it's Nick, do you? He always wants publicity for the band, but he wouldn't give up his family, would he?"

"I don't think Nick would do that."

"I hope not. Oh, I got a response from Tina." She held her phone so they could both read it.

"OMG! I heard from her too. Thanks for letting me know. Don't worry. Talk soon. Say hi to Walter."

"I thought so," Walter said. "Did she say what newspaper she works for?"

"It's a woman's magazine. I can't remember the name." She furrowed her brow. "What was it?"

"That's better than a newspaper. Maybe it won't make it into the mainstream news."

"Oh, my gosh! What if she calls Nick? Someone should tell him not to say anything."

"I think he has the sense not to talk to a reporter about his family," Walter said.

"We're talking about Nick," Lisa reminded him.

"That's true." Walter frowned. "I'm sure Tina is on top of things. Let her handle it. We're still on vacation."

"You're right. Tina will know what to do," Lisa agreed. "Let's go back. I think I'm going to buy that pretty skirt."

They strolled back to the vendor hand in hand, each pondering the implications of an article published about them in a magazine. What would the consequences be? Would people ask for their autographs? Would the North Pole be invaded by tourists? And who were these mysterious sources who knew them but had betrayed them?

4 *Silly Girlfriend*

"What's that sound?" Nick picked his phone up from the bar. "I got a text from Tina."

"Two more beers?" the bartender asked.

"Yeah," Kris answered, gulping down the last drops in his glass.

Nick read the text. *"Reporter contacted me for an interview about our family. Don't talk to her! She wants to know about the N Pole. Let me know if she calls you. Tell her you don't know what she's talking about & hang up!"*

"When are George and Tina coming back from Boston?" Kris asked.

"In about a week."

Nick didn't understand why Tina was so worried about this. What was the big deal? So what if someone found out their identities. Besides, if she did an interview, it could promote the band. Publicity was good, but he had no intention of talking to anyone about his family. It would be embarrassing for people to find out who he was and would diminish his message. Still, he'd never understood why it was such a big secret. Who cared?

"Your parents are funny," Kris said.

"My parents are intense, but not in a good way." Nick paid for the beers the bartender had placed before them. "They don't get it. They don't get like how vital my music is. It totally wakes people up from their brainwashed lives."

"Your father's face gets red just like my father's." Kris let out a loud guffaw.

"That's why he had a heart attack. He can't deal with stress."

"I could've run the North Pole," Kris boasted. "I just like music better, like you."

"My parents jammed me my entire life about the business," Nick griped. "I'm so sick of it. It was all about the kids and toys. I'm sick of toys."

"Yeah. My father made me manage the Kringle Café at the Pole."

"What we're doing is much more important." Nick sipped his beer. "We're getting the message out to the masses to wake up. We're all puppets of the corporatocracy."

"Yeah, puppets." Kris chugged his beer.

"Hey, go easy on that, dude." Nick shook his head. "Even the band doesn't get it. They think I'm too political and that we're going to alienate people. But I don't want passive fans. I want hardcore fans who get it. We need a revolution!"

"Yeah!" Kris nodded vigorously.

"You get it," Nick said. "I'm glad you're on my side."

"Right on," Kris said. "I get it because we're cousins. By blood."

"You know what?" Nick demanded. "Let Tina have the North Pole. She's into it. It's her thing."

"Let Tina have the North Pole!" Kris yelled, raising his glass.

"Keep it down," Nick urged. "We don't want anyone to know about that."

"I hate the holidays," an older woman sitting at the bar slurred.

"They suck," Kris agreed.

"It's just a materialistic greed fest promoted by the big companies that really run the world," Nick intoned. "We have to open our eyes."

"What?" She scowled and shook her head.

"Most people don't get it," Nick said in a low voice to Kris. "The message is in the music."

"In the music." Kris nodded.

***

"I like your sister," Tina said to George as he drove.

"She likes you too. So does my entire family, as I

knew they would." He parked the car alongside the curb. "This is where I went to high school."

Tina looked at the large brick building. "High school seems so long ago, doesn't it?"

"Well, a lot can happen in four or five years."

"Once we leave home, it seems like we grow up pretty fast."

"That's true. I wanted to go to college, but I became a musician instead."

"What did you want to major in?" Tina wondered.

George shrugged. "I've taken a few classes just for fun. I like history and philosophy and finance."

"Finance?"

"Yeah, just to learn how to invest my money. It's a good thing to know."

"I agree with you." Tina nodded. "But what does it mean when you go back home? I ended up back at home. Isn't that a step backward?"

"It depends on why you go back. If you go back to live with your parents because you can't make it on your own, that's one thing, but you went home for a different reason," he pointed out.

"But it's a safe choice," she said. "I don't have to finish college if I don't want to or go out and find a job. Don't you think it was too easy for me? Isn't that a bad thing?"

"I wouldn't call what you've gone through easy," George said. "You had lots of opposition from your own family and had to fight to stay. Besides, it was an honorable thing to step in when your father had his heart attack."

"I guess."

"Why do you doubt yourself?" he asked.

"I don't know. I think the call from that reporter is making me reassess things and question myself."

"But you love your job. You love it at the North Pole."

She smiled. "I do love it. I guess I'm being silly."

"Okay, silly girlfriend. Let's get some coffee for me and tea for you. It'll warm us up." He pulled away from the curb.

"Actually, hot chocolate sounds good."

"I like the sound of that," he said. "I also want to talk about us, about our relationship."

"What about it? The distance? I know it's a problem when I'm at the North Pole and you're in Florida or on the road." Tina bit her lip. She was good at figuring out solutions, but this one baffled her.

"Distance is just an obstacle," George said. "Though it would be nice to see each other more often."

"I don't want you to suggest quitting the band again," Tina warned. "That's not an option."

"Okay. I'll keep it in mind for the future, but right now, I just want to discuss our level of commitment," he said. "Remember how impressed we were with Lisa and Walter when they promised to be completely honest with each other?"

"Yes. We said we'd do the same thing."

"So, in that spirit, I want to talk about what we each want from this relationship. Is that okay?" He glanced at her as he drove.

"Of course." But this made her nervous.

George went through a drive-through and ordered two hot chocolates to go. Tina held the warm cups in her hands while he found a scenic spot and parked.

"I didn't want to go inside because I wanted to talk," he explained.

"Okay." She carefully sipped the hot chocolate.

He turned in his seat to face her. "I think it's pretty obvious how I feel about you, since I wanted you to meet my family."

Tina's blue eyes met George's brown ones as he spoke.

"I want you to know that this is serious for me. I love you, and I love everything about you, and I'm totally committed to making this work."

"Okay." She looked down at her lap.

"Am I going too fast?" he asked. "I don't want to scare you off."

"No, not at all." She looked into his dark eyes again. "I feel the same way, George."

"Good. I've never felt this way about anyone before," he confessed. "I wish our jobs didn't keep us apart."

"I think making a commitment to each other and spending as much time as we can together is all we can do right now," Tina said. "Someday, we'll probably have to live at the North Pole because that will be my job until I can pass it on to one of my chil..." She stopped and felt herself blush.

"*Our* children," he corrected. "Our daughter will carry on your family tradition one day."

"I think we're getting ahead of ourselves. Right now, we just need to figure out how to spend more time together."

"It's important to make a serious commitment to each other, especially with the distance, and I'm not afraid to talk about our future," George said fervently.

"Me too, but I think it's better to talk about our immediate future right now rather than way in the future," she rationalized.

"Okay," he said slowly. "But we can do a little more than make a commitment to see each other whenever and I want to ask what you think..."

"Oh, George. I do love you and want to be with you all the time. I really do," Tina blurted. "It's just difficult to think about all this. Soon I'll be back at the North Pole again and we'll be apart. And what's going to hold us together?"

"That's what I wanted to talk about. It might be crazy, but I think..." He hesitated.

Tina felt tears threatening to appear. She always tried to keep her emotions in check, but she suddenly found herself overcome. She reproached herself to stay focused on the present moment and not worry about the future day when they'd have to part again. She held the tears back and looked at him with shiny eyes.

"I'm sorry. What were you saying?"

George had a funny smile on his face. "This is harder than I thought it would be. But I think... I know it's crazy... but I hope..."

"What is it? What's crazy?"

"Well... What I want to say is... Will you marry me?"

A gasp escaped her. And then the tears overflowed. This was the last thing she'd expected at this moment. She'd often feared the distance would cause them to drift apart from each other or prove to be too difficult.

"George! Oh, my gosh! Of course. Yes! Oh, my gosh!"

Tina wiped away the tears that streamed down her face with her hands. She wondered whether she had a tissue in her purse. She couldn't believe this was happening. Her heart was filled to the brim.

"I love you so much," she murmured to George.

They leaned toward each other and kissed. Tina couldn't stop shaking. She hoped she wasn't dreaming.

"I wanted to buy you a ring, but I'd rather pick it out together," George said. "We can go look at rings right now if you want to."

"You planned this," she accused with a smile.

"I've been so nervous about it," he admitted. "I wasn't sure what you'd say."

"How could you not be sure?" Tina marveled.

"I was afraid you'd want to move more slowly because of the distance thing," he said. "We won't be able to live together all year round yet."

"Yes, but now we've made a promise to be together and to be true to each other. And we have a foundation to build upon."

George beamed at her. "I'm so happy. I can't wait to tell my family."

"Oh! I have to call my parents," Tina realized.

***

"Hey," Nick said as he leaned on the bar. "What do you think of Isabella?"

"She's hot, but I like Lilliana. Do you think she likes me?" Kris asked hopefully. "*Rock Goddess* is the best band ever."

"Except for my band, *Black Ice*," Nick corrected him.

"Right on."

"But do you think she likes me?" Nick asked.

"Lilliana?"

"No. Isabella."

"Why wouldn't she? You're totally awesome," Kris responded.

"Right." Nick nodded. "Have you noticed how Loren is always bothering her?"

"Yeah. Always massaging her feet and making her laugh. What a jerk," Kris said. "She's probably just being polite."

"Right. I bet that's it. He's being totally unprofessional."

"Totally."

"Loren is George's friend, you know," Nick told Kris. "He's a good guitar player. I'll give him that. Our manager, Robin, is the one who thought we needed another guitarist, but I was like, 'the Beatles only had four guys and they did just fine,' you know?"

"Totally." Kris finished his beer.

"They had a George and John and we have a George and John," Nick pointed out.

"And Milo and you and Loren," Kris added.

"And our George is vegetarian, just like their George, and then we got discovered by a great manager. It's meant to be. What do you call that?"

"Luck?"

"No. Destiny. It's our destiny."

"I'm hungry."

"Me too. Let's get a pizza," Nick suggested. "I wish George would get back so we could rehearse. I can't wait for him to get over my sister so we can get back to band business.”

“I thought he was visiting his family.”

“He is, but he wanted her to meet them.” Nick rolled his eyes. “Then he wants to run up to the Pole or have her visit, and he’s not making the band a priority.”

“Better to be free and single like us,” Kris affirmed.

“Especially when you’re a rock star. It’s a better image for the band. We’re these edgy rebels that can’t be tamed.”

“Isn’t John getting married to Courtney this summer?”

“Right. The next thing you know, he’ll be quitting the band to get a regular job and have kids.” Nick shook his head. “Love sucks.”

“It totally sucks, but do you think Lilliana likes me?” Kris asked again.

“Sure. But why tie yourself down?”

“She totally likes me, doesn’t she?” Kris nodded. “Hey! If John quits, I could join the band.”

“Can you play the guitar?”

“No.”

“Can you play *any* instruments?” Nick raised his eyebrows.

“No, but I could learn. How hard could it be?” Kris shrugged.

Nick shook his head and finished his beer.

***

“Mom!” Tina shrieked into the phone.

They were still sitting in the car and Tina had her phone on speaker.

“What? What happened?” Clara asked with alarm. “Your father fell asleep watching TV again. Let me turn it off… Okay, what’s wrong? Are you okay?”

“Nothing’s wrong, Mom. George asked me to marry him.”

Tina couldn't help herself as tears filled her eyes again. George handed her a napkin.

"That's wonderful, Tina!" Clara exclaimed. "We just love George. When did this happen? Let me wake up your father. Dear... wake up. Tina's on the phone. She has good news."

"Don't wake him up," Tina said. "It just happened. You're the first to know. I have you on speaker. He's right here."

"George? Congratulations you two. I already felt like you were part of the family. This is such merry news."

"Thanks, Mrs. Claus," George said. "Luckily, your daughter said yes."

"And why wouldn't she? If she didn't, I'd have her head examined," Clara said. "Goodness. Did you decide on a date? We have to start planning."

"We haven't discussed any details yet." Tina looked at George and shrugged.

"We can figure everything out later. Now, what does the ring look like? Take a picture with your phone and send it to me."

"We're going to pick out the ring together," George answered. "I want Tina to choose what she likes."

"Okay. Send me a picture when you get it."

"I will, Mom. We haven't even told George's family yet."

"Oh, George's family. We're going to have to meet them," Clara said. "Now George, I know this is difficult, but you can't tell your family who we are."

"I know. I understand."

"Good. Whew! This is so exciting. I have to tell Myra. She can help me plan. Her daughter got married last year. There's so much to do. I don't know where to start."

"Mom, I'm going to get off the phone. I just wanted to tell you right away. We'll talk more about it next time," Tina promised.

"Okay. Bye. Oh, your father's waking up..."

"The mall has a nice jewelry store," George said when she hung up. "Do you want to look at rings?"

"Yes!" Tina giggled.

Neither of them could stop smiling as he drove to the mall. Tina had been afraid that he'd see how impossible their situation was and want to cool things down, but the fact that he was ready to make this commitment despite their obstacles meant that he really did love her. She was bursting with joy.

"So, one little thing," he said as they drove. "I hope you're not too attached to the idea of getting a diamond ring because I read this article about slave labor in the diamond industry. They're using children to mine..."

"Children? That's terrible!" Tina cried. "George, I don't care what kind of ring I have, as long as I have you."

"Well, you do, and I'm glad to hear you say that." He beamed.

"Nick will be proud of us for not buying a diamond," she said. "He's into causes."

"Yeah, and I agree with his messages most of the time. The other guys give him a hard time about it, but he's not wrong. He's just a little extreme," George said. "But I have a feeling he won't be too happy about this."

"Why not?" Tina asked with surprise. "You're his best friend and he's been okay with our relationship. He must know this is serious."

"He's been acting cool about it, but he has this idea about our band image. He thinks we should all be single bad boys, you know?" He shrugged.

"But isn't John getting married this summer?"

"Yeah. He's not too thrilled about it, and now we're going to tarnish our image further." George laughed. "Maybe he'll kick me out of the band."

"That would solve everything, wouldn't it?" Tina smiled. "But he'd never do that, and I don't want him to. You love being in the band and I'd never make you choose."

"I know." George squeezed her hand. "We'll make it work."

5 *Happy or Not*

"Where should I drive?" Lisa asked. "I have no idea where I'm going."

"Just go straight." Walter peered at the map. "The sanctuary should have signs."

"I'm going to pull over," she said. "I have to get my water. It's in the back."

Lisa pushed her oversized sunglasses back up on her nose and carefully pulled onto the shoulder in the shade. There were ruts everywhere, and she didn't want the jeep to tip over.

"Look. We can see the water from here. It's such a pretty color."

"Do you want to walk down there?" Walter asked.

"Not right now. I'm getting sunburned." She gazed in the ocean's direction. "It's so peaceful."

"I'm really glad you came on this trip with me," Walter said. "I enjoy being with you."

"I enjoy being with you, too." She smiled fondly at him.

"Are you ready to take this to the next level when we go back?" he asked.

"What next level?" Lisa reached behind them for her water bottle, finding it rolling around on the floor.

"You know, we talked about living together at the Pole," he reminded her. "Remember, we agreed to be totally honest with each other? If it's too fast for you, that's fine. Just tell me the truth."

Lisa gazed into Walter's eyes. He had beautifully expressive eyes with long lashes and dark brows. She'd found his beard and mustache sexy, though he'd shaved for their vacation. She knew she could be herself with him and she felt cared for and secure.

"I don't know." She took a sip of water. "It's not like I have to give notice to Tina when I move out, but your place is a little small for me. I know it's built for someone your size, but I just feel big and clumsy when

I'm there."

"Hmm." Walter nodded. "I guess I never gave it much thought. I see your point. I could probably change some things to make it more comfortable for you. Why don't we see what we can do when we get back?"

"That's a good idea." Lisa squeezed his hand. "You're really important to me, Walter. You're the best guy I know, and I want to keep moving forward with you. I really do. I've just never... It's a little..."

"It's okay. We'll talk more about this later. The most important thing to me is that you're happy with me."

"Yes, I am. Very."

She leaned toward him, and they kissed. His lips were warm and soft and inviting. She forgot about everything else until her phone rang.

"Darn it! It had better not be that journalist lady again." She looked at the caller ID. "It's Tina. Hello?"

"Lisa, I'm so glad you answered the phone."

"Tina! I feel like I haven't seen you forever. Is that journalist still bothering you? What did your parents say about it?"

"Oh, I forgot all about that. I don't think she's called my parents. I texted Nick and told him not to talk to her."

"How's Boston?"

"Cold..."

"Too bad you're not here. It's beautiful. Nice and warm..."

"Lisa! I have to tell you..." Tina interrupted and took a deep breath. "George proposed and we're getting married!" She shouted into the phone.

"Shut up! Oh, my gosh! You almost broke my eardrum." Lisa turned to Walter. "They're getting married."

"When?" he asked. "Tell her congratulations."

"Walter says congratulations. When did all this happen? When are you getting married? Do you like his family?"

Tina laughed. "It just happened today. I'm still in shock. I can't believe it. I'm so happy. We haven't even talked about when or where or anything," she gushed. "His family is great. He has a cute little nephew, and I met his grandmother. She's so sweet. And I like his sister. They're all great."

"Wow. You know I hate you because you're so happy. You just totally blew my mind."

"I know, right? Oh, my gosh. How are things with you guys? Is everything going well?"

"Yeah, everything's fantastic. As a matter of fact, we were just talking about moving in together," Lisa answered. "But you know me. I run from happiness."

"Oh, Lisa, I want you to be as happy as I am," Tina said earnestly. "You can do it. Walter is a wonderful guy."

***

"This is great news!" Gloria grabbed Tina into a hug. "We're so happy."

"Congratulations," Grover said.

"I knew it!" G.G. laughed.

"Welcome to the family." Gemma smiled. "Does Garrett know yet?"

"No, I'll call him later," George replied.

"Let me see your ring." Gloria took her hand. "Oh, it's lovely."

"I didn't want a diamond. I really like the light blue color of this stone and the Swarovski crystals around it are so pretty," Tina said.

She couldn't stop staring at her ring. The blue stone was a soothing color, and the crystals sparkled around it.

"Stunning," Gemma said. "And nontraditional."

Tina went over to G.G. on the couch and held out her hand.

"Now, isn't that beautiful?" G.G. commented.

"Congratulations to both of you. I'm so pleased."

George sat down next to G.G. and Tina sat beside him. She tried to stop staring at her ring. Adrenaline raced around inside her and she could hardly sit still.

"When's the big date?" Gloria asked.

"Where are you going to live?" Gemma wondered. "I know Tina lives up north somewhere."

"We haven't decided anything yet," George answered. "Tina's parents live in Florida and so does her brother, Nick. I guess we have to look at our work schedules and see when wedding plans would fit in."

"I wish Grandpa were here to see this," G.G. murmured.

"Me too," George said.

"Tina, have you told your parents yet?" Grover asked.

"Yes, I called my mother, but I haven't told my brother yet. My parents love George and they're thrilled."

"Well, I look forward to meeting them," Gloria said. "I wish they were closer."

"It would make things easier," Tina said.

"Have you decided whether you're going to get married here or in Florida?" Gloria asked. "I just want to know so I can find out what's available for the reception."

George and Tina glanced at each other.

"We haven't decided yet," he said.

"Do you want a big traditional wedding, Tina?" Gemma asked. "Or do you want to keep it small with just family?"

"I really haven't thought about it." Tina shrugged sheepishly.

"Every young girl dreams of her wedding," G.G. declared. "You must have some idea of what you want."

"I guess I have to think about it," Tina answered.

Actually, Tina *had* dreamed about her ideal wedding when she was younger. It was when she and

Kai had been dating in high school. They'd known each other since they were children at the North Pole because their parents were friends. She'd dreamed of a Winter White wedding with crystal ice sculptures and imagined the two of them in a sleigh pulled by reindeer as they went off on a romantic honeymoon. She'd been head over heels about Kai until he'd run off to Geneva after graduation. He hadn't been ready, and it had broken her heart.

When he finally returned to the North Pole, it was too late. She'd already met George. But she'd felt a flutter in her heart at the sight of him, and it had weakened her. She was thankful she'd been able to resist... sort of.

Her dream wedding had been about Kai, and it had been nothing but a fantasy. And now she'd spin new dreams with George that would come true.

Tina sat beside her perfect fiancé, surrounded by this close-knit family that she'd soon join. It was a little complicated because they didn't know who she was, but she and George would work it out together. And right now, her heart was full and she couldn't be happier.

***

Nick wasn't happy. Isabella had insisted that Loren play rhythm guitar on the song Nick had written for her called "Rock Me." Lilliana was playing lead guitar and his drummer, Milo, was playing drums. Kris had swept the floor of Milo's rehearsal room to protect Isabella's bare feet. How was he supposed to get close to her with Loren always lurking around flirting or joking with her and offering foot massages?

Nick was sure she was interested in him, despite Loren's incessant flirting. The attraction between them was almost palpable, like jolts of electricity arcing between them. She was probably just trying to arouse his jealousy by using Loren. It was all a crazy game.

Well, two could play at that.

"Nick?" Isabella said.

She stood in front of the mic, looking over the lyrics. Her long dark hair curled down to her waist.

"Yeah?" He stumbled over a wire on the floor in his haste and heard Loren quietly chuckle.

Isabella began to softly sing the words he'd written.

"You dance as gracefully as the breeze
That rustles gently through the trees
My imagination may run away
But I hope you will stay..."

"That's right," he said, remembering the first time he'd sung it to her on the patio at his rented house.

"I think we should change this line." She pointed her graceful finger. "I think it sounds better if it says, 'But I hope with me you'll stay.' It flows better. What do you think?"

"Right. Change it."

Nick became aware of her subtle scent. He hoped she'd see how much they inspired and complemented each other. They'd written a great song together called "Frozen Dreams," which merged their two styles in a perfect blend. He was edgy hard rock, and she was a melodious dream. That didn't sound synergistic, but it worked and gave each of their bands crossover fans. Robin, their manager, seemed convinced, and Nick hoped that meant that they could continue to tour together.

"Thanks, Nicky," she smiled at him flirtatiously.

Nicky? She'd never called him that before. She had a pet name for him. That meant something. He smiled smugly and glanced at Loren, who stood talking with Lilliana. They both had their guitars slung over their shoulders at the ready. Milo tapped the drums impatiently.

"Hey, everybody," Isabella said. "I want this to be

collaborative. Everybody has good ideas, so before we get into the studio to record this song, does anyone have any suggestions?"

"Yeah. I got one. Right in the middle, we can change the bridge like this." Lilliana played a short solo.

"Beautiful." Isabella nodded. "Loren, can you add anything to that?"

"Sure can, but I think the lyrics in the chorus are weak," he said. "No offense, Nick, but they need more emotion. You know, more passion." He looked directly at Isabella.

Nick felt anger and indignation rising. His first reaction was to defend his lyrics and tell him to back off from her, but Isabella was encouraging input. Loren was a thorn in his side that he'd have to learn to ignore. The last thing he wanted to do was let Loren know he was getting to him. Even though he was. Big time.

"I think it sounds sick," Kris declared. "You and Isabella write awesome songs. You should write more together."

"Thanks, Kris," Nick said gratefully. "See? He represents our typical fans, and he's into it."

"Hmm." Isabella frowned. "That's good, but I agree with Loren that we need to make the chorus stronger."

Loren looked at Nick and shrugged.

Nick realized Loren had given him an opportunity to get closer to Isabella. He leaned toward her, inhaling, and pointed to the chorus scrawled on a page. He hated to admit it, but Loren was right. It was weak.

"We can work on it and make it better," Nick said.

"Crazy nights and lazy days
Your love has me in a daze
Chase me through a dark maze
And I'll reveal all my ways..."

"You want more passion." Nick scribbled on the page.

"Wild nights and lonesome days
I find you hidden in a maze..."

"Good," Isabella said. "I like the feeling that evokes." She took the pen from him and added a line.

"And fight the nightmares that remain..."

Nick contemplated the words. As he took the pen back, her touch made his heart quicken. He wrote the last line.

"And fantasies flourish unrestrained..."

Isabella gave him a pleased smile. "That's good." She turned her attention back to the page. "Let's change 'flourish' to 'flower.' What do you think?"

Nick nodded. "It works."

"I like it," she said happily. "This is better. Great job, Nick." She gave him a quick hug. "Let's run it through with the new lyrics and the new bridge."

"I can add to it," Loren assured her. "I can do anything you want." He gave her a meaningful look.

Isabella let out a giggle while Lilliana rolled her eyes. Nick involuntarily coughed. He was trying to form the words in his head to ask her out after rehearsal. He could mention something about working on their songs. It was a good excuse.

"Hey, Isabella, let's go get a drink and something to eat when we're finished here," Loren said and dramatically strummed his guitar.

"Okay." She glanced at Nick as she answered.

Nick turned and went back to his mic, where Kris was setting up a music stand for his notebook so he could read the lyrics.

"Hey, don't we have plans later?" he asked Kris loudly.

Kris looked at him with surprise. "Yeah. Okay."

Nick's phone rang, and he was happy at the interruption. He saw it was Tina. He pondered how he could make it sound like it was another female in front of Isabella. She had to learn that she was lucky to have his attention, and that Loren was the wrong guy for her. Nick needed to ignite her fervor for him.

"Hey," he said into his phone in an overly friendly manner.

"Nick, it's me," Tina said. "Hope you're not too busy. I just wanted to..."

"Wow, sorry I didn't call you back. Things are happening with the band," he said.

"I didn't call you before," she answered with confusion. "Anyway, I just wanted to tell you..."

"Right. I'm already busy tonight, but maybe another time."

"What are you talking about?" Tina asked. "It's me, your sister."

"Don't be bummed," he continued. "I promise I'll call you soon."

"Nick, just listen a minute," Tina said. "I have some news. I just wanted to tell you that George and I got engaged. I wanted you to know."

"Wow, really? Wow."

Nick shook his head in disbelief. What was George doing? Where were his priorities?

"I hope you're happy for us," Tina said, feeling annoyed.

"Right. Yeah, I am."

"Good. I already called Mom and Dad. We'll be back next week. You sound distracted, so we'll talk more when I get back. Okay?"

"Right."

"I'm so happy, Nick. I know I don't say it much, but I love you."

"Right. Love you too." The words came out before Nick realized it. He looked up to see Isabella staring at him. She cleared her throat and adjusted her microphone.

"Was that an obsessed fan?" Kris asked.

"Just some girl," Nick said, hoping everyone could hear him. "They call me all the time."

6 *Nicky C*

"Who was that on the phone?" Kris asked, gulping his beer. "Was it a groupie?"

"It was Tina."

Nick felt down and stared into his beer. Isabella was out somewhere with Loren right now and he was sitting here with Kris.

"But I thought you said it was some girl."

"I was trying to make Isabella jealous," he confessed. "Tina told me they got engaged."

"Isabella's engaged?"

"George and Tina," he answered irritably. "Now almost half the band will be married and ruin our edgy image."

"Don't worry. There's still you and Milo and Loren. None of you even have girlfriends."

"I wish Loren would get married and quit the band," Nick grumbled. "I wouldn't mind if that happened."

"Maybe George will quit the band and move up to the Pole," Kris mused.

"That would suck. We need George. Am I the only one dedicated to this band? My *life* is this band. Everything else comes second," Nick declared.

"Yeah!" Kris enthusiastically agreed. "Don't worry. I won't leave over some lame girl."

"Right. I'd never give up the band either. I don't care who comes along." Nick shook his head. "It's like those mermaids who tempt sailors into the water to drown. What are they called?"

"Mermaids?"

"No, they're called something else." He furrowed his brow. "Sirens. I think they're called sirens. Yeah. I'm going to write a song about it."

"A song about mermaids?"

"No, about sirens. I'll call it 'Song of the Siren.' What do you think?"

"You could call it 'Sound of the Siren,'" Kris

suggested.

"Then people will think of a loud noise like an ambulance siren. These sirens are like evil mermaids that lure men to their deaths."

"That's scary, dude."

Nick sighed heavily. "But I know Isabella likes me. It's obvious. You can see it a mile away."

"She's totally into you. She'd be crazy not to be," Kris said. "I mean, you're Nick Claus!"

"Hey, keep it down," Nick cautioned. "I go by Klaus here. Got to keep a low profile."

"Why? Because of stalkers?"

"You've never hung out anywhere except the Pole, huh? It's different everywhere else. People don't believe in Santa. They think he's a myth. We can't reveal who we are or they'll think we're whacked."

"They don't believe in your father?" Kris looked confused. "But he's real."

Nick shook his head. Sometimes his cousin was a little dense.

"Anyway, I want to be known as Nick, the rock star, not Nick, Santa's son. Got it?"

"Yeah, because Tina is Santa now," Kris said, nodding.

"And she can have it."

"Yeah!" Kris suddenly bellowed. "Hey, you should have a cool nickname like Nicky C and I could be Kris K for my last name, Kringle. Pretty dope, huh?"

Nick remembered when Isabella had called him Nicky. It had given him a warm, funny feeling. What were she and Loren doing right now? It made him crazy to think of them together. He was going to have to do something about it. He just had to figure out what.

"Pretty dope, huh?" Kris repeated.

"I'm not going to be Nicky C." Nick scowled.

Only Isabella could call him Nicky. He couldn't wait to hear her say it again.

"It's weird that our fathers are brothers, but we

have different last names." Kris scrunched his brow. "What's up with that?"

Nick shrugged. "It has something to do with the whole mythology of our family. I don't care about that stuff."

"Me neither."

Two young women approached them at the bar. "Are you from *Black Ice*?"

"Yeah, we are," Kris answered.

"I told you!" one of them squealed to her friend. "We're big fans."

"This is so sick," her friend enthused. "We saw you in concert when you played with *Rock Goddess*."

"It was the best concert!" the first one shrieked.

"Thanks," Kris said. "We tour with them a lot. I know Lilliana and Isabella."

"Cool!" the second one cried.

"Kris, go out to the car and get them some T-shirts," Nick ordered, handing him the keys. "I have some boxes in the trunk."

"You're the singer," one of them said.

"Right."

"You're my favorite. The way you scream into the microphone is so... just so..."

"Who's your new guitarist?" the other interrupted. "I don't remember him from your first CD. He's new, right? The blond guy."

"Loren," Nick mumbled.

"Is he here?" She glanced around. "He's so good. I really like him."

Nick groaned inwardly.

***

"I like to braid hair," Gemma commented. "This French braid is going to look pretty on you. I love the way your hair feels. It's so silky. You're lucky to have such beautiful hair."

"Thanks." Tina perched on the window seat with her back to Gemma. "I wish it was thicker like yours."

"Don't tell anyone, but I was hoping Garrett and Tonia would have a little girl so I could fix her hair. But they had a boy, and Tonia's hair is too short. Everyone has dark hair. You're the only one with light hair. I wonder what color your kid's hair will be." Gemma laughed. "I'm getting ahead of myself, aren't I?"

"I wonder that myself."

Tina frowned as she thought of the possibility of having a daughter with dark hair. How could she take over as Santa if she had dark hair?

"There you go." Gemma patted her back.

"George told me you're a writer." Tina turned to face her. "What do you write?"

"Oh." Gemma looked toward the window. "I like to write fiction. My stuff falls under the Literary Fiction genre." She gave a little laugh. "But I don't know how literary it is."

"I like to read. I'll have to read some of your books," Tina said.

"Don't feel obligated. Only read them if you want to."

"I will. I spend a lot of time flying. It's the perfect time to read."

"You know I grew up with two brothers and I was so excited when Garrett got married because I thought, now I have a sister." Gemma sighed. "But Tonia's a teacher and she has Evan, so she's pretty busy and there's not much time to hang out. And now you're joining the family, but you live too far away. I can't win."

"It would be fun to hang out. I wish we were closer," Tina agreed.

"Well, the good thing about my job is that my schedule is flexible. So once you guys get settled, I can come visit," Gemma said brightly. "I'd like to see your toy company. I bet it was fun growing up around toys."

There was no way Gemma could visit and discover who she was. How was she going to keep George's family away from the North Pole?

"It wasn't as much fun as it sounds. My father was a workaholic and gave more of his attention to my brother because he thought Nick would take over the business," Tina explained.

"Ha! You sure messed with his patriarchal dreams, didn't you?" Gemma grinned. "Girls can do anything now. Isn't it great?"

"Yes, we can."

Tina recalled how she'd had to fight to maintain control of the North Pole. Nick hadn't been interested in his birthright, but Uncle Kris had and assumed his son was next in line. Tina had never intended to step in. She'd never considered the possibility until her father's heart attack had necessitated it. Then she'd learned that not only was she good at managing the business, but she loved it. She already understood how it worked from helping every season since she was a kid, and now she discovered she enjoyed the challenges. She enjoyed finding ways to improve production and foster teamwork. She loved the elves and the reindeer and the idea of putting smiles on all the children's faces. She believed in her work. She believed in the North Pole.

"You're smiling," Gemma observed. "It's great to love your job. I love what I do, too. It's nice being your own boss, isn't it?"

"It sure is," Tina agreed.

"Both of our brothers are rock stars," Gemma said. "The desire to be creative is in our genes. Even Garrett is creative working as a chef. You and Tonia have more practical jobs. Teaching and running a business."

Tina's phone rang, and she picked it up without looking at the caller ID to see who was calling.

"Hello?"

"Santina Claus? This is Jill Graham from *Modern Woman's World* magazine again. Please don't hang up or make me say that again," she implored. "I talked to your assistant, Lisa. My sources..."

Gemma got up and indicated that she was leaving the room. Tina nodded.

"I'm sorry. I think you have the wrong number. I don't know what you're talking about."

"Let's not play this game. I think it's time that your family came out of the shadows. People need the optimism of Santa nowadays and just think how inspiring it would be for little girls to know that Santa is now a woman. I really hope that you consider giving me an exclusive interview," Jill implored.

"Uh..." Tina wasn't sure what to say. "I'd really like to know who keeps telling you that I'm..."

"Trust me. My sources are solid and I guarantee I won't reveal who or where you are," she promised. "I realize it would put your family in a difficult position, so I can do the interview anonymously with no pictures, if that's what you prefer."

"I still don't know why you..."

"Please think about it. I just want to give people some background on your family and let everyone know that the reins have been handed to a woman, so to speak. This is historic and I want the exclusive," Jill insisted. "I personally guarantee anonymity for you and your family."

"I'm sorry, Jill. I hope you find this person you're looking for, but it's not me." Tina hung up.

She couldn't imagine who Jill's source could be. Unless she was bluffing. Perhaps she'd figured it out somehow, or was pursuing a shred of information she'd discovered somewhere. Jill sounded pretty confident in her information and she'd somehow acquired their private phone numbers, but she couldn't have any proof. And she had no story without Tina's cooperation. Hopefully.

On the other hand, it could be a good thing. Jill was correct that people needed a little more optimism and positivity in their lives. Tina thought of Evan telling her that his friends didn't believe anymore. How sad. And it certainly *would* inspire little girls. Was it written in the family history that their cause had to remain secret? Everyone knew them at the North Pole, and it had always been forbidden to reveal their identities to the outside world. She'd never questioned it. But times had changed.

Tina dialed her parents' number. It rang three times, and she almost hung up.

"Yes, Tina. This is your father. Your mother is making scones," Santa said. "I hear congratulations are in order. George is a fine young man."

"Thanks, Dad."

How on earth was she going to broach this subject with her father? She wished her mother had answered the phone.

"Your mother is very excited. She can't wait until you get back to begin planning."

"Yes. It will be fun," Tina said distractedly. "Uh, Dad, I wanted to ask you something."

"Of course, I'll walk you down the aisle. Now I don't know if you should let Nick's band play at the reception. They don't play the right type of music."

"Yes, that's true, but I wanted to ask you something else." Tina was beginning to lose her nerve. Her father had always intimidated her.

"Well, what is it? Your mother wants to talk to you," he said impatiently.

"Um, I know that our family has always been anonymous..."

"Now, your mother was talking about this," Santa said. "If George's family wants to place an announcement in the local paper there, then you can use our alias, Klaus. That's perfectly fine."

"Okay, but what I wanted to ask you was..." She hesitated. "Well, have you ever given any interviews, you know, anonymously?"

"What kind of question is that? You mean about who we are? Of course not. What would be the point?"

"I was just wondering…"

"Absolutely not."

"Okay, but George's little nephew told me that his friends said there's no Santa Claus. I think that's awful, and maybe it's time to renew people's belief in the magic of Christmas," Tina blurted. "You know, give people something to believe in again."

"What have you done?" he demanded.

"I haven't done anything," Tina answered. "I just thought that maybe anonymously…"

"Absolutely not," he repeated adamantly. "I won't allow it. Here's your mother."

"Tina, is there some kind of problem?" her mother asked tentatively.

"No, Mom. I was just asking Dad if he's ever done an interview. I thought it might be a good idea to do one anonymously. I was just telling Dad that George's little nephew told me his friends don't believe in Santa Claus, and I think that's terrible," she rambled. "It would be nice to renew people's belief…"

"I hear you, Tina, and I understand what you're saying," Clara said evenly. "But under no circumstances should you ever do an interview. We've gone to great lengths to stay behind the scenes. The focus isn't on us. It's about the children."

"I know, but they don't believe anymore. Everyone is so cynical."

"Yes, that's true, and I see your point. I really do, but it's not a good idea."

"Okay, Mom. Don't worry. It was just a thought."

George came in and sat on the window seat beside her, giving her a quick kiss.

"I'll see you next week. I have to go, Mom."

"You never sent me a picture of your ring," Clara reminded her.

"I'd rather you see it in person," Tina said.

"Okay. I guess I have to wait. See you soon."

Tina disconnected the call and turned to George.

"That journalist called me again. She said she could do an interview anonymously and that it would give people hope and optimism."

"Did you tell your parents she contacted you?"

"No, but I asked them what they thought about doing an interview and they're not receptive to the idea at all." Her shoulders slumped.

"This journalist knows who you are?"

"I didn't confirm it, but she seems to know."

"Are you considering it?" he asked.

"I don't know." Tina shook her head. "After what Evan told me his friends said, well, I wish I could let people know that it's all real. Our family is real, the elves are real, the reindeer are real, the magic is real. I want kids to believe in us. It just makes me sad to think that they don't."

"But kids aren't going to read an article."

"No, but their parents will, and if parents believe, they'll help the kids believe again too," she reasoned. "But I don't know. What do you think?"

He shrugged. "I think it's something that you should consider carefully. Once it's out there, you can't take it back."

"You're right. It's probably better to leave things as they are." Tina gave him a little smile. "I'm glad I can talk to you about this stuff and we have no secrets."

"Well, how do you know? I could be the Easter Bunny." George grinned.

"I'd like to see that." She giggled at the thought.

They both stared out the window at the bright, snow-covered yard below. Tree branches were bowed under the weight of the snow and a squirrel ran across the yard.

"Who do you think could be her source?" George asked.

"That's the question." Tina frowned. "It can't be any of us, but how else could she have our phone numbers? It doesn't make any sense."

"I have to admit, it was a big surprise when I found out who you were. I didn't believe it until I saw it with my own eyes," George said. "I guess I stopped believing when I grew up, just like everybody else. I don't know why we lose our belief in magical things. It's like the world becomes colder and harder and reality kind of hits you."

"That's awful."

"But you didn't have that happen to you because you lived it," George realized.

"I guess I'm lucky." Tina shrugged. "I felt neglected by my father because he was such a workaholic and was more interested in Nick because he thought he'd carry on the family legacy, but no one has a perfect childhood."

"What you do helps." George put his arm around her. "You bring joy to so many children."

"That's my job." Tina smiled.

"And you made a believer out of me," George said. "I believe in you, Santina Claus."

7 *Dilemmas*

"Do we have to go back?" Lisa groaned. "I like it here."

A gentle breeze blew off her straw hat and she bent down to pick it up, causing her lounge chair to tip her into the sand. She burst out laughing.

"Are you okay?" Walter asked with concern.

"Yeah." She stood and brushed herself off. "I'm just a klutz." She straightened the chair. "Let's take a walk along the beach."

"Okay." He got up, adjusted his hat, and took her hand. "Now you know why I want to retire here someday. But not yet. I like my job and I enjoy working for Tina."

"What was it like working for her father?"

"Santa?" He pushed his sunglasses up on his nose. "He was grouchy. I used to let him vent. He really couldn't talk to anyone else except Clara, of course. But I think he got burned out. It's a tough job."

"What did he vent about?" Lisa wondered.

"Mostly, he worried about Nick not being interested in the business. It never occurred to either of us that Tina would be the one to take over when he retired. Funny, huh?"

"I remember when I first met her and she told me that her parents had a toy company. I thought that sounded fun and I didn't understand why she was reluctant to work there." Lisa shook her head. "Little did I know."

Walter chuckled.

"She told me that her father was a workaholic and she couldn't talk to him," Lisa recalled. "She's still intimidated by him."

"Yeah, he's difficult to talk to sometimes."

"I don't have any trouble. He doesn't scare me."

"Maybe not, but I scare you," Walter teased.

She frowned. "You know it's not you. Relationships

scare me. You know I have a crazy history."

"I don't care." He tugged on her hand and she leaned down to kiss him.

"I have to admit I'm nervous about living together, Walter."

"Why? We're getting along great."

"I know, but we're opposites in so many ways."

"Like what?"

"Well, you like to get up early and I like to stay up late. I have to drag myself out of bed to go to work." Lisa thought. "And you're quieter than I am. I like to be around people and talk to everyone. You're more private."

"I don't think those things are a problem," Walter said.

"I'm always bumping into things at your house."

"That's because my house is arranged for someone my size. We can fix that," he assured her.

"And you're a total neat freak like Tina. I know I drive her crazy sometimes. She wants things just so," Lisa said. "Actually, it drives *me* crazy because she can be a perfectionist. You're a little like that, too."

"That's because everything should be put away in its place. That way you can find it again, and I don't like clutter."

"We might fight about stupid things like that," she cautioned. "Sometimes couples break up over minor issues."

"We won't let that happen," he vowed.

Lisa remembered that his ex-wife had left him for someone else.

"A lot of couples end up breaking up over stupid things. You know? Minor differences can escalate."

Walter stopped walking, and they stood gazing out at the aqua blue water. The waves were gentle, and the sand was warm beneath their feet.

"Beautiful, isn't it?" He grasped her hand tighter. "I want to share things like this with you. I want a future with you, and I won't let anything stupid break us up. I promise."

"I hope not, Walter." She sank down onto the sand, and he sat beside her. "I wonder when Tina and George are going to get married. And where? Do you think they'll get married at the North Pole?"

"I don't know. They'll have to work it out with their schedules, and I don't think George's family knows who she is. That'll be tricky."

"I bet *they* don't have any stupid issues to deal with. Tina is too perfect. I hate her," Lisa grumbled.

"I'm sure they have their differences and you don't hate her."

"You're right, but I don't think they've ever had an argument," she marveled. "I can't imagine it. They'll probably be one of those couples who always agree on everything and make you sick."

"Tina isn't perfect. She made a fool of herself with Kai a few times," he reminded her.

"That's right!" She giggled. "She was a total fool around Kai."

"I'm glad everything worked out with George and I'm happy for them," Walter stated.

"Me too." Lisa sighed.

***

"This is a problem," Clara said as she sat on the couch with an open magazine on her lap. "I always imagined Tina would have a traditional North Pole wedding. But she was with Kai then."

"Hmm." Santa sat staring at the TV from his comfortable recliner chair. He was having trouble staying awake.

"We had such a lovely wedding here in Florida and then a second ceremony at the North Pole. I always wanted Tina to have a traditional Winter White wedding, but that probably won't happen now," Clara said. "I guess Nick too, but I can't picture him being married. I suppose it could happen. I wonder if there's ever been a single Santa? Of course, then you wouldn't be here, dear. But maybe one of them was initially single. Can you imagine? How would you date someone? What would you say when they ask you what you do for a living?" She shook her head.

"Hmm."

"I don't know how we're going to have a wedding with George's family without them knowing who we are, although I guess my family never knew," she continued. "I wonder if Tina and George have discussed this yet. They might decide to get married in Boston. Do you think that's what they'll do?"

"Hmm."

Clara gasped. "I just thought of something. I know Tina will want Walter there, and he should be. She's always been close to him. But they might wonder why there's an elf at the wedding. I guess they'll just assume he's a little person. That pointy-ear thing is a myth. I wonder how that got started."

"Hmm."

"Where do you think they're going to live? Probably at the Pole whenever George isn't on tour and then here in Florida for a few months after the season ends. That would make sense, except it would create a conflict with the band. George would have to be here to rehearse and record and go on gigs or whatever they do. Nick wouldn't be thrilled if he was gone a lot." She shook her head again.

"Hmm."

"Isn't there another band member who's getting married? I thought Nick had mentioned it. Wouldn't it be ironic if this whole music dream of Nick's fell apart because of Tina's wedding and he decided he wanted to take over as Santa after all? Oh, my goodness. You don't think that could happen, do you? Tina is doing such a good job."

"Hmm."

"Probably not. He was never interested in our work. That's fine, but it bothers me that he doesn't seem to respect it. I don't know where we went wrong. He has a very negative attitude about the business and Christmas, for that matter. Doesn't he realize what a wonderful service we provide? I think it's essential, really, especially with all the cynicism in the world today. It's just a shame." Again, she shook her head.

"Hmm."

"There might be some good recipes in this magazine. What do you feel like having for dinner?"

"Hmm."

"Dear, what do you feel like?"

"Huh? What?" Santa's expression was blank.

"You haven't heard a word I've said, have you?" Clara accused.

"I was listening."

"Then what did I just ask you?"

"Uh... something about something..."

"That's what I thought. Why do I waste my breath?" She shook her head again. "This entire family tunes out from each other. Goodness, I don't even know what I'm reading. What is this?" She flipped back to the cover. "Myra likes this magazine. *Modern Woman's World.*"

"Anything."

"What?"

"Make whatever you want for dinner. It's always good."

"Oh, so you're starting to like this healthy food, are you? It's not so bad, is it?" Clara smiled. "I knew you'd come around if you tried it."

"It's okay."

"You know, I noticed something. You don't get recognized anymore since you lost weight."

"I shaved."

"But it's more than that. Losing weight made a big difference," Clara remarked. "Do you think Tina will become a vegetarian like George? Who would've thought we'd all become vegetarians?"

"Hmm."

"Goodness. We've gone through so many changes in the last few years. We even have a female Santa now. I never would've believed it, but I think it's great. Girls really can do anything. Now if I could just get you to cook once in a while..."

"Hmm."

"George is such a great addition to this family. I really like him, don't you? I can't wait to meet his parents. I bet they're just as nice. Things seem to be going so well. Nick's band is successful. Who would've thought? I had no idea he was so talented. And the business is running smoothly. Tina is happy. Everything worked out. All that worrying for nothing. I tell you I spent some nights tossing and turning, but now things couldn't be better. I guess I should knock on wood, huh?"

Clara tossed the magazine onto the coffee table and bent over to give the wood a quick rap just as the remote slipped from Santa's hand onto the rug with a thump. He let out a rattling snore.

"Typical." Clara let out a sigh.

***

"I like your family, especially little Evan. He's so cute."

Tina peered out the window of the plane at the fluffy white clouds and then down at her ring. It felt so good on her finger. She clasped George's hand. There were so many good things ahead.

"I knew they'd love you. And Evan followed you around like a little puppy. He wouldn't leave your side." George grinned.

"Little kids must sense my Santa energy." She smiled at the thought.

"We should talk about the wedding," George said.

"I don't really want a big wedding. I just want our family and close friends there, people who are important to us."

"That's probably wise considering who you are. I just want my family and the guys in the band there. Knowing my parents, though, they'll probably want to invite everybody they've ever met."

"Did your brother have a big wedding?"

"I thought it was too big. It's not what I would want. I just want to be married to you. All of that other stuff isn't important to me."

"Me too," Tina said. "It's a little delicate because of my family. I mean, my uncle, Kris Kringle, and his wife will be invited, but I guess I can't invite any of the elves." She bit her lip. "I have to invite Walter."

"Invite anyone you want, and we'll worry about explaining it later," George assured her.

Tina shifted in her seat to face him. "I don't think we thought this through. I always assumed I'd get married at the North Pole. It's not really a big deal. We can get married anywhere, but the fact that your family doesn't know who I am makes things complicated. I never considered how secretive we'd have to be."

"We'll figure it out."

"I'm sorry, George."

"Don't apologize for who you are," he said. "I love who you are. I love you."

"But where are we going to live? I need to be in one place and you need to be in another."

"I need to be with you," George emphasized. "Don't worry. Things will get easier."

"Gemma wants to see the business. What are we going to tell her?"

"I know it's complicated. She'll just have to visit us in Florida." He shrugged. "Don't worry so much. We'll work it out."

"Where do you think we should get married?"

"Well, either my family will have to fly to Florida, or your parents and the band will have to fly to Boston. No matter what we do, somebody is going to have to travel," he said.

"Maybe we should pick a neutral place," Tina suggested.

"Like where? Vegas? Hawaii?" His smile broadened. "We could just elope."

"Oh, I don't think our parents would like that."

"It's not their wedding."

"I know, but I don't want to deny them the chance to be there with us," Tina said. "Why don't we have it in Boston? That way, G.G. won't have to travel."

"Don't worry about G.G. Her knee will heal and she'll be fine. She's not that old, and she likes to travel."

"I still think we should have it in Boston."

"Okay. But what about the honeymoon?" he asked. "We don't have to take anyone else into consideration. It's just you and me."

"I like the sound of that." Tina leaned over to give him a kiss. "I always wanted to take a vacation in Hawaii. How about you?"

"Hawaii it is."

"Ow," she cried out.

"What is it?" George asked.

Tina pulled off her shoe and began rubbing her foot and toes.

"I have a cramp in my foot. I get them sometimes."

"Here." He took her foot in his lap and began massaging it. "It could be a lack of vitamin D. We'll get some sun in Florida."

"Thanks. That feels better." Tina gazed at George with affection. She was so lucky to have such a great guy.

"Do you take supplements?" he asked with concern. "You don't get any sun up north."

"Most of our food is fortified with vitamin D."

"That's good. The natural source is always better.

We'll make sure to get outside a lot before you have to go back."

"Okay." Tina admired her ring again. "We're going to have to choose a date so our parents can start planning."

"The sooner, the better," George said. "Let's just get married right away. Why wait?"

"You mean as soon as we can get things planned?" Tina asked.

"I can't wait to be married to you. Let's just do it as soon as possible. We can have the reception right at my parents' house. We'll tell them we want to keep it small. What do you think?"

Tina's head spun with details. It was all happening so fast. She squeezed George's hand.

"Yes," she said. "I can't wait to be married to you, too."

8 *Rings and Things*

"Hey, welcome back, man," Nick said, grabbing one of George's suitcases when he entered the house and placing it by the stairs. "Kris, take these upstairs."

"Leave it, Kris," George said. "I'll bring them up later. I just want to rest a little. Traveling is stressful enough, but our flight got delayed because of the weather in Boston."

"Bummer," Kris said.

George sank onto the couch. "I love my family, but it's a family frenzy whenever I visit."

"Family frenzy," Nick repeated. "Good title for a song."

"I like it," Kris enthused.

"Yeah. I'm glad they got to meet Tina," George said.

"So, you and my sister, seriously? Aren't you rushing into things?" Nick asked.

"Come on. You know we've been involved for a while. It was never a casual thing. I thought you'd be happy for us," George said.

"Right. Congrats, man. It's cool," Nick said.

"Yeah. Congrats," Kris echoed.

"Thanks," George answered.

"But you and John are messing up the band's image," Kris declared.

"What do you mean by that?" George asked.

"Nick said that you guys are supposed to be bad guys that rebel against the masses?" He frowned and glanced at Nick.

"That's not what I said." Nick shook his head. "Our image is that we're edgy bad boys. You know, we're spreading the message of freedom and revolution to our followers. We've got to talk the walk."

"Walk the talk," George corrected. "You make us sound like a cult."

"Yeah?" Nick looked pleased.

"You think having band members who are married

will ruin our edgy image?" George shook his head.

"Well, it's hard to be edgy when you have to ask your wife if you can go out on tour. Like you have to ask permission to play with your friends."

Kris snickered.

"Then you'll have kids and quit the band. It's the beginning of the end," Nick ranted. "You guys are getting tamed."

George shook his head. "I thought you'd be happy for us. I was going to ask you to be my best man."

"I'll do it," Kris offered. "We'll have a wild bachelor party."

"No, I don't want that," George said. "I just want you guys to come to the wedding and be happy for us. I won't desert you, Nick. We started the band together and I'm with you. Nothing will change except I'll be married."

Tina was right to insist he stay in the band. He felt a little guilty for considering giving it up and abandoning Nick.

"Right," Nick said doubtfully. "When's the big day?"

"That's what I have to talk to you about," George said. "What gigs do we have coming up? Is there a break in the schedule?"

Nick pulled out his phone. "Let me check. We need to get back into the studio, and Robin is lining up another tour. He's trying to work around John's wedding date."

"When's that?"

"June. Courtney wanted the whole traditional thing." He shrugged. "Maybe you can get married around the same time."

"We'd like to do it before then," George said. "We're not having a big wedding. We just want to get married as soon as we can arrange it."

"Are you going to live at the North Pole?" Kris wondered.

"We'll split our time between here and there. And

we want to plan a honeymoon too before we have to be separated for a while."

"Honeymoon? This is really happening," Nick groaned. "I was hoping I was having a flashback."

"Nick, you don't do drugs and I thought you said you were fine with this." George rubbed his face with his hand and yawned. "You realize we're going to be related, don't you? You'll be my brother-in-law."

"That's cool, but, like, this is blowing my mind. I'm still trying to wrap my head around it," Nick said.

"Me too," Kris added.

"Wow. I just realized Santa will be my father-in-law," George said with awe.

***

"Your ring is just stunning," Clara said, holding Tina's hand up to look at it again. "Isn't it, dear?"

"For the hundredth time, it's very pretty," Santa said from his recliner.

"Well, I can't stop looking at it since we picked them up at the airport," she said. "Now Tina, I still don't understand why you didn't get a diamond. I know George said something in the car about miners, but don't they have to mine all gemstones?"

"I guess so, but George says that they use slave labor at the diamond mines, including children," she explained. "If he says it, I believe it. Besides, I love the blue stone in this ring."

"It's terrible that such things go on in the world." Clara shook her head. "Anyway, I'm glad you like George's family. I can't wait to meet them."

"You won't have to wait too long because we want to get married as soon as we can."

"What?" Santa suddenly pounded his fist on the arm of the chair. "What's the rush? Are you getting married because you have to?"

"Dad! Of course not," Tina objected. She felt herself

blush. "We just want to be married before I have to go back to work, that's all. Why wait?"

Clara patted her hand. "Just give us enough time to plan a nice wedding. This is something you'll remember for the rest of your life. I went online yesterday to check out venues..."

"Oh, Mom. We decided to get married in Boston," Tina interrupted. "We can all fly up there. They have a big house and can put us up. I just didn't want to make George's grandmother travel. She had knee surgery."

"Okay, if that's what you want," Clara said with disappointment.

"We don't want a big wedding. It's just not us and we'd prefer something small with just family and close friends there." Tina shrugged. "But you can help me shop for a dress. I want to find something long and lacy."

"Oh, that'll be fun." Clara clapped her hands. "I know a bridal shop right in town. Myra and I already went there, and I saw this beautiful, long white dress with little beads..."

"I don't want a white dress, Mom." Tina sighed. "I'm tired of white. There's so much white at the Pole. I think I want something off-white, cream-colored, you know, old-fashioned looking. Maybe even something pastel."

Clara sighed. "I'm sure they'll have something you'll like."

"This isn't the kind of wedding I always dreamed of," Tina admitted. "But I'm marrying someone who isn't from the North Pole and his family doesn't know who we are, so we have to do things differently. But it doesn't matter. Being married to George is the most important thing." Tina felt her eyes brim with tears. She still couldn't believe it.

"Of course it is." Clara pulled her into a hug.

Tina wiped away her tears with her fingers. "Oh, my gosh. I think I've been holding in all these emotions. I'm just so happy."

"I know, sweetie. We're just thrilled. We love George. Don't we, dear?"

"Hmm."

"Oh, I have to call Lisa so they can fly here instead of going back to the Pole after their vacation," Tina remembered. "There's so much to do. We have to choose a date once George talks to Nick about the gigs they have lined up for the band."

"Why don't you get married in a few months or during the summer, so we have time to plan things?" Clara asked. "There's no rush. Planning is part of the fun, isn't it?"

"Are you sure you don't have to get married?" Santa asked suspiciously.

"Dad! We also want to have time for a honeymoon before I have to get back to work and we won't be able to see each other for a while, probably months. I'll be back home and he'll be here working with the band. We just want to solidify our commitment before we have to be apart."

"Where are you going on your honeymoon?" Clara asked.

"We were thinking about Hawaii." Tina smiled. "Doesn't that sound wonderful?"

"You might as well just stay here in Florida," Santa said. "We have beaches here."

"That's true," Clara agreed. "We could put you up in a nice hotel right on the beach. That's what we did."

"Thanks, but I've always wanted to go to Hawaii." Tina sighed at the thought of being alone with George in a tropical paradise. She couldn't wait.

***

"Vacation over. Back to reality, huh?" Lisa said in the front seat of the car. "Where's George?"

Tina turned on the blinker to change lanes. "He's at a band rehearsal. Nick is freaking out a little because he thinks George is going to quit the band."

"Didn't he tell you that last year?" Lisa asked. "You said he was considering it because you were apart so much. He was going to move up to the North Pole."

"Who's moving up to the North Pole? I can't hear back here," Walter groused from the back seat.

"George said he might quit the band," Lisa turned to tell him.

"No, he's not quitting the band anytime soon," Tina said, glancing at Walter in the mirror.

"Good. That would really upset Nick," Walter said.

"Geez, you're going to blind me with that ring," Lisa commented. "Could you have found anything sparklier?"

"It's the Swarovski crystals," Tina said. "Aren't they beautiful?"

"Are you going to wear a tiara too?" Lisa giggled.

"I'm glad you two had a nice vacation." Tina spoke loudly so Walter could hear her.

"Yeah, and we didn't even fight once," Lisa said.

"Everything was perfect," Walter agreed.

"We're even talking about the L word."

"L word?" Tina repeated.

"Yeah, *living* together," Lisa clarified.

"I thought the L word was L-O-V-E."

"Oh, we're way past that." Lisa waved her hand. "But don't even mention the M word."

"Which one is that?" Tina asked.

"You know, what you and George are doing."

"Oh."

"And it's not only me," Lisa continued. "Walter went through a tough divorce, so he's not ready for that either."

"I can understand that," Tina said. "So, Walter, I'll drop you off at Nick's first. Then Lisa and I will head over to my parents' condo."

"That sounds great. It's nice of Nick to let me stay at his place again."

"Nick always enjoys seeing you," Tina assured him. "I think they're planning a guy's night later in the week."

"Uh oh. That means we're having a girl's night," Lisa warned.

"You'd better not get me into trouble." Tina smiled. "I always get into trouble when you're around."

"What are friends for?" Lisa poked her shoulder.

"Tina, tell us about your plans for the wedding," Walter said.

"I get butterflies every time I think about it," Tina confessed. "We're all flying to Boston a few days before the wedding. Robin chartered a plane for us. We're just going to have the ceremony and reception right at George's parents' house. Did I tell you that his brother is a chef? He's going to make all the food."

"And his family doesn't know who you are?" Walter confirmed.

"No, they don't."

"Then what happens when George is at the North Pole with you?" Lisa questioned. "What happens when you have little white-haired babies?"

Tina shrugged. "I guess we'll cross that bridge when we come to it."

"Oh, my gosh. We have so much flying to do. We have to go up to Boston and then back to the North Pole. I hate that long flight."

"I know. George and I are flying to Hawaii from Boston. Then I have to go back to the Pole and it'll be months before I see him again," Tina bemoaned.

"That'll be hard," Walter said sympathetically.

"Yes. I can't stand being apart, but we have no choice." Tina sighed as she pulled into the driveway of Nick's house.

"Wasn't Nick talking about buying a house?" Walter asked.

"That's right. He's been working with a realtor and George was thinking about buying a place for us here."

"I remember when Milo lived here with Nick and

George before he bought his house," Lisa recalled.

"The band has come a long way in just a few years," Walter said.

"That's for sure," Lisa said.

"I have the key. The guys are at a rehearsal at Milo's," Tina said, popping the trunk.

"Good. I just want to take a nap right now," Walter yawned as they exited the car.

"I feel energized, but it's probably adrenaline," Lisa said. "I bet I crash tonight, though."

She pulled Walter's suitcase from the trunk while Tina unlocked the door. They entered the darkened, quiet house, and she handed the key to Walter.

"We'll see you tomorrow," Tina said. "George made you guys a casserole for tonight. He said to just put it in the oven. He left you a note."

"That's great. I'm starving." Walter yawned again.

"See you tomorrow. I'll miss you." Lisa leaned in to give him a kiss.

"I'll miss you too," he said. "We got used to being together all the time. It'll feel weird to be apart."

"I know." Lisa pouted.

"Have a good nap," Tina said.

She and Lisa went back to the car and got in to head to the condo.

"It's great that you and Walter are getting along so well. I'm impressed," Tina told her.

"Oh, my gosh. He's driving me crazy," Lisa blurted.

"What? I thought you were getting along," Tina said with surprise.

"Don't get me wrong. I'm happy with Walter. I really am, but we've been together twenty-four hours a day and I just need a break."

"Okay." Tina backed out of the driveway.

"Don't you judge me," Lisa admonished. "You just wait until you spend every minute with George. He'll start to get on your nerves."

"I can't imagine that."

"You begin to notice all the little quirks and habits about someone and, after a while, it starts to irritate you. I don't know." Lisa shook her head. "I've never lived with anyone. Maybe I'll get used to it. I'll probably adjust."

"Does this mean you want to live with him or not?" Tina wondered.

If Lisa stayed with her at the North Pole, then she and George would never be alone when he visited. That would be awkward. She'd have to kick Lisa out for those visits and make her stay with Walter. On the other hand, living alone in the apartment in between George's visits would be lonely. But she shouldn't be selfish. She truly wanted Walter and Lisa to be happy together.

"I'm not saying I don't want to live with him," Lisa clarified. "I love Walter. I really do. He's the best guy I've ever met, besides George, of course. But I just think that people need time away from each other every once in a while, you know? Alone time or time with friends to balance things out."

"That makes sense. I think you're right that it takes time to adjust to living with someone. You have to change your habits and get used to theirs," Tina said thoughtfully as she drove. "But we both lucked out with these guys."

"Big time." Lisa nodded vigorously.

9 *Celebrations*

"Here's to George." Loren raised his shot glass.

"George!" the guys shouted, downing their shots.

"Tina's great," Walter stated.

"To Tina!" the guys shouted.

"You're not losing a sister; you're gaining a brother." Milo slapped Nick on the back.

Nick lurched forward and spilled beer on the carpet.

"Oh, man," he grumbled.

"We'll clean the carpet later," George promised.

"And soon we'll be losing John too," Milo announced.

"Here's to John!" Loren raised his beer bottle.

"To John!" they all responded and took a swig.

"We'll miss him," Milo said.

"We're just getting married, not moving to Siberia," John protested.

"You guys are ruining the band's image," Kris remarked, pouring more shots. "But you don't have to worry about me, Nick."

"You're not part of the band," Loren pointed out.

"Neither is Walter," Kris retorted.

"That has nothing to do with it." Loren rolled his eyes. "Whether or not you're married has nothing to do with the band's image, anyway."

"Thanks, Loren," George said.

"Right on, brother." Loren raised his beer bottle.

"Walter's the only one who's been married here," Nick pointed out.

"And he's divorced. What does that tell you?" Milo guffawed.

Walter frowned and took a sip of his beer.

"Tell us some scary stories, Walter. Tell us what George and John are in for." Milo grinned.

"I enjoyed being married, if you want to know the truth, so don't look at me," Walter responded.

"You're just a softy," Milo accused. "Nick, do your

song. Nick wrote a song for George and John."

They downed their shots, and Nick picked up a guitar. He pulled a folded paper from his pocket and looked at Milo, who nodded to urge him on. He began with a simple strum to accompany his words.

Girls are sugar and spice
And everything is nice, nice,
They run away and we pursue
It's an innocent game we play too, too

Opposites like a magnet attract
Making us whole in the ways we lack, lack
Until we catch them and are caught
And we realize what we've wrought, wrought

Milo stood by him and sang the chorus with him.

Friends, don't get sucked into the abyss
Because she'd rather be Mrs. than Miss
Don't get tricked into a life of submission
Begging for freedom and asking permission

Nick continued with his lyrics as Loren chuckled.

Life will change with the words 'I do'
You'll find you're a victim of a coup, coup
The battle of wills has only begun
If it's not too late, I advise you to run, run

Love is a game that you will lose
This is the arena they choose, choose
To control our every move and break our will
To train us like dogs until we're over the hill, hill

Learn to say 'yes dear' and you'll be fine
If this is your choice, then stay in line, line
Or grab your freedom and be a man

And run away as fast as you can, can, can

Milo again sang the chorus with him. Then he stood back and clapped.

"Bravo, Nick."

"If you add a bridge, you could put that on one of our CDs," Loren said.

George looked at John, who shook his head and said, "You guys are jerks."

"They're just jealous," Walter said.

"Have a sense of humor." Milo poked John. "Besides, I think he speaks the truth. You guys have temporary insanity, and one day you'll wake up and wonder what you've done."

"That's not true," Walter said. "Don't listen to them."

"You're still bitter because Tiffany broke up with you," John told Milo.

"Not true. I broke up with that crazy chick," he retorted.

"They're *all* crazy chicks," Loren said.

"Amen." Milo clinked beer bottles with him. "May we never fall into the abyss."

"That's a good name for the song," Nick noted, writing on his paper.

There was a knock on the door and they all turned in that direction and then back to each other.

"I'll get it." George pushed himself up from the couch.

He crossed the room to the front door and pulled it open. Robin, the band's manager, strode into the room.

"Congratulations, George. You too, John. I brought a few gifts." He set a bottle of whiskey and a bottle of tequila on the coffee table. "I hope nobody's driving tonight."

"Nah. We've got plenty of room here," Nick assured him.

"Nick wrote a song for the guys," Kris said. "Play it

again, Nick."

"Yeah?" Robin raised his eyebrows at him.

"I don't think we need to hear it again right now," George said.

"Then let's have a toast for these two lucky guys," Robin suggested. He opened the tequila and poured shots on the stained coffee table.

"Do we have any limes and salt?" Walter asked.

"Don't be a wimp, Walter," Loren said. "We don't need no stinking slimes and salt. I mean limes and salt."

They raised their shot glasses.

"To money years of happiness for George and John," Walter pronounced.

"Ha! You said 'money.'" Kris laughed.

"I think you guys are way ahead of me." Robin grinned as they downed their shots.

"I can't stay long." Robin wiped his mouth with the back of his hand. "Got to get home to the family."

"See?" Milo demanded and nudged John.

"I have something else in my car for you." Robin went back outside and returned, holding a large piñata shaped like a rooster. "It was all I could find, but I filled it with goodies. Where do you want it?"

"Outside!" Loren called out. "Let's do this on the patio."

"Let's do this!" Kris yelled.

They stumbled outside into the darkness. George flicked on the outside light. "We need some rope."

"We don't have any rope," Nick stated.

"I have bungees in my car," Milo said and went to retrieve them.

"Now we need something to hit it with," John said.

"Let's just punch it," Loren suggested.

"I'll punch it," Nick offered.

"Hey, the guests of horror go first," Loren insisted.

"You mean honor," Walter corrected with a laugh.

"That's what I said," Loren slurred.

"I'll punch it!" Kris yelled.

Milo returned with the bungee cords, and they worked to attach it to a beam that extended over the far end of the patio. The bulb by the sliding glass door cast a dim halo of light into the darkness. After much fumbling, they managed to attach it and it swung garishly from the beam. John staggered up and took a swing at it. The brightly colored rooster swung wildly and hit him in the head. Everyone roared with laughter.

"You're up, George," Robin said.

George stepped up and took his turn without doing much damage. The guys each took turns until they all attacked the rooster at once, tearing it to shreds and releasing an avalanche of condoms.

"Perfect!" Loren yelled.

"I've got to go." Robin watched them scoop up the scattered condoms.

"One more shot," John shouted.

"Can't do it. I'm driving," Robin responded.

They trailed behind him into the house, blinking when the light hit their eyes.

"Don't get too crazy, guys," Robin advised.

"Thanks, Robin." George hugged him while John hovered, holding a beer bottle.

"Tina and Courtney are lucky ladies," Robin stated before disappearing out the door.

***

"Oh, my gosh. I spilled my wine," Lisa cried. "Sorry, Mrs. Claus."

"Call me Clara." She sopped up the wine with napkins on the dining room table.

"We should take a picture of our rings," Courtney said.

She held her hand with polished red nails and a large diamond ring on her finger next to Tina's. She wore a tight red top and skinny black jeans. Her long, dark hair was a direct contrast to Tina's white hair as she snapped a photo with her phone.

"I don't know why you didn't insist on a diamond. It's traditional," she said. "I'm doing everything traditionally. I wanted the whole thing, you know? The big wedding and everything that goes with it."

"George said the diamond mines use child slave labor and we didn't want to support that kind of thing," Tina said, feeling defensive. "We're just having a small wedding with close family and friends."

Courtney shrugged and sipped her wine.

"Have you found a dress, Courtney?" Clara asked.

"Oh, I found a hella bridal gown. It's open in the back with a big bow just below the waist and has little sequins all over the front. It's sick." She smiled. "And it has a long train and a totally wicked veil."

"Sounds lovely," Clara said. "We found a beautiful dress for Tina."

"What does it look like?" Courtney asked, tapping her nails on the table.

"It's a pretty antique off-white color with lace at the collar and on the sleeves. It has an empire waist and lots of lace. I just love it," Tina enthused. "It was exactly what I wanted."

"It sounds Victorian," Courtney commented.

"Yes, it's old-fashioned. I love that style," Tina answered.

"It's a pretty cream color. Tina didn't want to wear white," Clara said.

"You have to wear white!" Courtney exclaimed. "It's like a tradition."

"People can have whatever kind of wedding they want," Lisa said. "What about your honeymoon? Where are you guys going?"

"We're going down to Mexico. My parents have a place in Puerto Vallarta."

"That sounds nice," Tina said.

Clara refilled their wineglasses. There was a knock on the door as they sipped.

"Come in," Clara called.

The door swung open, and Myra entered. She had short, curly red hair and a big smile. She set two wrapped boxes on the table.

"Hi, girls. Sorry I'm late. I had to make popcorn for our husbands while they watch the game or whatever they have on TV."

"I hope Nicholas doesn't fall asleep over there. He falls asleep every night in his chair." Clara poured a glass of wine for her.

Myra waved her hand. "Marty does the same thing. Maybe they'll keep each other awake or snore in sync."

They laughed and clinked their wine glasses.

"Myra, this is Courtney. She's getting married to John this summer. Her fiancé is in Nick's band with George," Clara explained.

"Congratulations to you, too. It must be contagious." Myra took a sip of wine.

"So, tell us the truth," Lisa said. "What's the secret to a long marriage?"

Clara and Myra looked at each other and burst out laughing.

"Let me think," Clara said, trying to keep a straight face. "You have to be able to talk to each other. Or at least, they have to listen."

"Let's face it," Myra said. "You have to put up with a lot of things that drive you crazy."

"That's the truth." Clara nodded.

"I knew it!" Lisa cried.

"But it's not all bad," Clara said, glancing at Myra. "We shouldn't give them such a bad impression."

"You're right. They'll find out on their own." Myra laughed again.

"You guys are a lot of help," Lisa said sarcastically.

"Men and women are different, you know. We have different priorities," Clara said. "It's nice to have someone to do things with and build a life with. You just have to learn to put up with another person."

"It helps to be in love and to actually *like* that person." Myra sipped her wine.

"It's really unexplainable. Every couple is different," Clara mused. "You know how your father is, Tina. He's very stubborn, and I had to learn how to handle that."

"Tina, I've known you since you were a baby. I just can't believe you're about to get married." Myra shook her head. "Do you believe it, Clara? Where does the time go?"

"I know." Clara nodded. "And Nick's band is going on tour again. They're getting more and more popular."

"Are you going with the guys when they go out on tour this time?" Lisa asked Courtney.

She shrugged. "It gets pretty boring. They're always doing sound checks or rehearsing or traveling somewhere."

"Don't you girls worry about groupies?" Myra wondered.

"Myra!" Clara scolded.

"What? It's a legitimate question."

"John wouldn't dare." Courtney pointed a finger at them. "And if he did, I don't want to know about it."

"Wouldn't it bother you?" Lisa asked.

"Not if I don't know. Duh."

"I trust George completely," Tina declared.

"Don't be stupid," Courtney said. "It's bound to happen sooner or later, but as long as they come home to us, it's cool."

Everyone exchanged looks.

"I need more wine." Lisa grabbed the bottle and poured more for herself and Tina.

"You've got to be realistic. That's how it is when you're married to a rock star." Courtney sipped her wine.

"I made a delicious chocolate cake. Let's have some of that." Clara went into the kitchen and returned with a decadent-looking cake. "Tina, get some plates and forks, will you? Oh, and the cake cutter."

Tina retrieved these items from the kitchen, and Clara cut the cake. A few minutes of silence followed while everyone savored a slice and murmured their approval.

"It's so weird that your entire family has white hair." Courtney stared at Tina's hair.

"It's genetic," Clara responded quickly.

"Well, I have to decide whether to live with Walter." Lisa finished the last crumbs of her cake.

"Who's Walter?" Courtney asked.

"He's my boyfriend. He's older than I am and shorter, but he's great. He's hanging out with the guys tonight." Lisa looked at Tina.

"He works for us. He's the foreman of the union," Tina added.

"Oh, you mean the little guy?" Courtney frowned. "I don't get it, but whatever."

"Did Walter ask you to move in with him?" Clara asked Lisa. "He's probably not quite ready to get married again."

"Walter is a great guy," Tina said to Courtney. "He's kind and sweet. Just a really great guy."

"That's right," Lisa said. "I'd be insane to turn him down." She looked at Tina again. "But you know how I am. I sabotage myself."

Tina suddenly grinned. "I think you should do it. Do it! Move in with Walter and let's celebrate tonight."

Lisa beamed. "This party needs music."

"Let me see what I have." Clara got up and went to the bookshelf next to the TV. "I have *Black Ice* CDs."

"No!" Lisa and Tina shouted.

"Put on some dance music," Courtney demanded. "Let's get this party going."

"I know! I have a dance playlist on my iPod," Tina remembered. "We play it at work sometimes."

"Yeah, except then we want to dance instead of work." Lisa giggled.

"Dance party!" Courtney raised her glass.

Tina got her iPod and plugged it into the stereo. She chose her playlist and turned up the volume.

"This reminds me of Zumba." Myra jumped up from the table. "Remember when we took that class?"

"That was a fun class," Clara agreed. "Let's see if we can remember some of those moves."

"Zumba dance party!" Lisa danced around with her glass of wine, sashaying over to Tina and clinking glasses. "I'm going to do it. I'm going to move in with Walter."

Tina nodded and smiled broadly as she swayed. She was filled with happiness. This was turning out to be a fabulous year with so many wonderful things ahead.

10 *Party Pooped*

Tina moaned. "I think I drank too much wine last night."

She dragged herself over to the couch to sit beside Lisa, who was shading her face with her hand.

"Why is the sun so bright?"

"I'll close the curtains." Tina got up and shuffled over to the window in her slippers.

"You're up." Clara came from the kitchen. "I don't feel like making breakfast, but we have frozen waffles if you're hungry. Drink some orange juice. It'll make you feel better."

"Are you hungover, Mrs. Claus?" Lisa asked with surprise.

"Don't be silly. We just stayed up too late, that's all. I'm just tired." She furrowed her brow. "I probably drank more wine than I should've, though."

"When did Dad come home?" Tina wondered.

"Don't you remember?" Clara asked. "He made us turn off the music and went to bed."

"Oh, yeah." The memory was fuzzy. "Is he still asleep?"

"No, he went out earlier to play golf with Marty."

"I think I hear your phone," Lisa told Tina. "Either that or my ears are ringing."

"It's probably George." Tina jumped up and hurried into the bedroom to find her phone. She saw it on the floor next to her bed and grabbed it before it stopped ringing.

"George," she said breathlessly.

"Santina? This is Jill Graham from *Modern Woman's World* magazine."

Tina groaned and slumped onto the side of the bed. She had a slight headache.

"Just listen to me for a minute, Santina," Jill implored. "I know who you are. There's no sense in denying it. I've already started the article, and I'm going to write it with or without your cooperation."

Tina sighed heavily, trying to sort out a response in her addlepated mind.

"I don't know if you read the magazine, but I did an article a while back called 'The Truth Behind the Fairy Tale' about Princess Ava of Wellstonia."

"I didn't read it, but it sounds like some kind of unflattering exposé," Tina responded.

"Well, we have to sell magazines." Jill gave a little laugh. "But we helped them raise money for their foundation." She cleared her throat. "Look, I have the greatest respect for your family and what you do. I really do. I think it will be incredibly inspiring for little girls to know the truth. They need to know that the sky's the limit. Or even beyond. You can be a part of that message."

Tina put her head in her hands and groaned again. She wasn't sure what to say.

"I did the fairy tale article because I don't want girls to be brainwashed. I don't want them to have these unrealistic romantic expectations that will disappoint them when reality hits them in the face. It does everyone a disservice," Jill explained. "But your story is inspiring for girls. I'll be honest. I hate all the emphasis on appearance and cooking in most women's magazines, so I try to find subjects that are a little more... liberating."

"Girls don't read your magazine," Tina pointed out.

"Yes, but their mothers do. And their mothers will influence their daughters and sons' attitudes toward women," she reasoned.

"It's too early for this kind of conversation," Tina mumbled.

"I left my number in earlier messages. Call me and we can discuss this further. I think this will be beneficial for everyone. You have my assurance that I'll be discreet."

"I have to go."

"If I don't hear from you in a few days, I'll give you another call," Jill said. "I don't want to publish the article without your input."

Tina hung up her phone. She knew what she had to do. She had to tell her mother. But first, she had to hear George's voice. He answered his phone right away.

"I was just about to call you."

"Did you have fun last night?" Tina asked.

"Yeah. The guys got a little rowdy," George answered. "Robin stopped by and that was nice of him."

"I'm sorry my father was so antisocial."

"That's okay. I invited him, but I didn't expect him to hang out and get drunk with us."

"I guess you're right."

"How was your party?" George asked.

"We had a great girl's night." She giggled. "We played music and danced, and it was really fun. Even my mother and Myra were dancing. They were showing us their Zumba moves."

He laughed. "Sounds like you had a good time."

"I have a little bit of a headache, though."

"Yeah, I'm wiped out. Now we have to clean up. You should see this place. There are condoms all over the backyard," George said.

"Did you say condoms?"

"Robin brought over a piñata filled with condoms." George chuckled.

"Oh, my gosh."

"It was raining condoms. They're everywhere."

Tina giggled.

"I miss you."

"I miss you too. So much." Tina bit her lip. "That journalist called me again this morning. I don't know what to do."

"She's sure persistent. What did you tell her?"

"I didn't know what to say. I couldn't think. She said she knows who I am, and she's going to write the story with or without me," Tina said. "I just can't figure out who her source could be."

"That's a good question."

"She was saying how inspiring this would be for girls." Tina rubbed her face. "I just don't know what to do. I'm going to talk to my mother about it."

"I think that's a good idea," George agreed.

"Okay, I'd better go get it over with." Tina took a deep breath. "I love you."

"I love you too. I'll see you later."

George hung up, and Tina sat there trying to come up with what to say to her mother. This would not be an easy conversation.

***

"Hey, John, grab some condoms before you go. They'll come in handy on your honeymoon." Loren let out a laugh. "Oh, man. That hurts my head."

"I think I have to get something in my stomach," Milo moaned. "Let's go out to breakfast."

"We should help clean up first." John frowned. "Look at this place."

"On second thought, I don't know if it's a good idea to eat." Milo put his hand on his stomach.

"You guys can go," George assured them. "We've got this."

"You sure?" John asked, scanning the room.

"I think we should skip rehearsal tonight," Nick said.

"We can clean this place up," Walter told them. "Go home and get some sleep." He was busy tossing beer bottles into a plastic trash bin.

"At least we can recycle those," George noted.

"Okay, if you've got it..." John followed Milo and Loren out the front door. "Thanks, guys. It was epic."

"Man, we trashed this place." Nick surveyed the living room.

"We can steam clean the carpet," George said.

"It's not that bad," Walter said. "I'll load the dishwasher."

"Did you see the condoms all over the patio and backyard?" George laughed.

Nick picked a packet off the couch. "They're even in here." He walked over to the sliding glass door and peeked outside. "Holy..."

"I'll get a bag and start picking them up," George offered.

"We have to wash the kitchen floor. It's pretty sticky in here," Walter called from the kitchen.

"That was some party." George grinned.

"It was epic, wasn't it?" Nick nodded. "Anything for you, brother."

"Hey, that song was a little harsh. Is that really how you feel?" George asked.

"Every word of that song is true," Nick answered adamantly. "I should've called it 'Love Sucks,' except I think there's already an old song by that name."

"That's a terrible attitude for my best man to have," George said. "I hope you're happy for your sister and me."

"Love sucks until you're in it," Walter said, coming back into the living room. "I was pretty bitter after my divorce. I never wanted to get into another relationship again. I felt too disillusioned."

"You were right," Nick said. "There are too many games, too many lies, too much betrayal..."

"Not when you meet the right person," George interjected.

"I don't believe in that soulmate crap." Nick smirked. "I'm happy for both of you, but I'm not going to let myself get sucked into domesticity. They won't get me."

George and Walter looked at each other, and George shook his head.

"I thought you liked Isabella," Walter said.

"He does," George said. "But so does Loren."

"Ah." Walter nodded knowingly. "Nick, you've got to fight for her. I think sometimes we give up too soon. I know I almost did with Lisa last year. We went through a rough patch, and I let my ego get in the way." He shook his head at the memory. "I could've lost her because we were both too stubborn, but she's the best thing that's happened to me in a long time."

"Walter's right," George said. "You've got to do everything you can and, if it doesn't work out, at least you gave it your best shot. You've got to take risks sometimes. It's worth it."

"And then you'll have no regrets," Walter added. "You don't want to look back, wishing you'd done more."

"She's just playing with me," Nick said. "Trying to make me jealous with Loren."

"She wouldn't bother if she weren't really interested in you," Walter pointed out.

"You think?" Nick asked. "Nah, I'm not going to make a fool of myself."

"Then Loren wins," George said.

"I should do it just to mess with him," Nick said.

George and Walter looked at each other again and grinned.

"I'm going out back to pick up the condoms in the yard," George announced. "They're everywhere."

***

"Why didn't you tell me about this sooner?" Clara asked. "We can't have a reporter exposing who we are."

They sat at the table, picking at their waffles.

"I thought she'd give up. I thought if I denied it, she'd have no story," Tina answered defensively, wringing her hands.

"What magazine did you say she works for?" Clara asked.

"*Modern Woman's World.*"

"That's the one Myra gets. It's a pretty good

magazine."

"She called me too," Lisa confessed.

Clara groaned and turned to Tina. "This is going to give your father another heart attack."

"Who could her sources be?" Tina wondered.

"It could be a disgruntled former employee. Have you fired anybody recently?" Lisa asked.

"We never fire the elves. You were there when I negotiated the United North Pole Workers union contract with Walter," Tina reminded her. "Even though production is more efficient, we didn't let anybody go."

"I hope she hasn't called Nick," Clara worried.

"I texted him after she called Lisa and warned him not to talk to her," Tina assured her. "I don't think she's called him."

"That's a good thing. Can you imagine if she interviewed him? It'd be a totally negative interview. He hates Christmas." Lisa sipped from her glass of water.

"No, he doesn't." Clara shook her head. "He grew up at the North Pole. He doesn't hate it."

"Mom, have you paid any attention to the titles or lyrics of his songs? He has a very negative view of the whole thing. He thinks it's materialistic," Tina said.

"Well, I knew he didn't want to take over when your father retired, but I think you're exaggerating when you say he hates it," Clara protested.

Tina and Lisa glanced at each other.

"Mom, he wrote a song called 'Jingle Hell.' It's one of their biggest hits," Tina reminded her.

"And 'Death of the Pines' and 'Frost in My Head' and 'Black Snow,'" Lisa added. "Oh, and 'Aftermath of the Snow.'"

"She gets the point," Tina said. "Anyway, he named the band *Black Ice*. It's pretty obvious how he feels."

"I thought he was just being ironic." Clara furrowed her brow. "His song 'Parental Overload' bothered me, but it never occurred to me he was so unhappy being a Claus." She looked crestfallen.

"Mrs. Claus, he's just working through his childhood issues through his music," Lisa said. "It's a healthy thing to do, and I'm sure he doesn't hate you and Mr. Claus."

"He doesn't, Mom," Tina reassured her.

"Your father was too hard on him." Clara shook her head sadly. "He just wanted him to assume the role of Santa, just as he'd done for his father. But the more he pressured him, the more he rebelled. It hurt your father for Nick to reject everything he'd worked for and believed in. We should've accepted that Nick was more interested in music. We just didn't know what to do if Nick wasn't going to run the business. The last thing we wanted was for Uncle Kris to take over."

"But it all worked out," Lisa said brightly. "Your answer was right under your nose, and now your daughter runs the company and delivers the presents on Christmas Eve."

"What would we have done without you?" Clara smiled at Tina.

Tina shrugged. "I enjoy it, but when I first left home, I rejected the whole thing, too."

"You did?" Clara asked. "Goodness, I had no idea."

"I never hated it like Nick. I just wanted to get out on my own and follow my own interests."

"And you ended up right back here," Lisa said. "I feel so thirsty. I must be dehydrated." She finished her water.

"I was happy when I found out about our family history and that Santa was supposed to be a woman all along," Tina said. "I didn't feel worthy until I read that."

Clara pressed her lips together for a moment. "I'm sorry, Tina. I feel like such a failure as a mother. I focused almost all my energy on supporting your father. You know how stressed out he was, but I didn't pay enough attention to you kids."

"Don't say that, Mom," Tina said. "You're a wonderful mother. The best."

"Thanks, sweetie." Clara reached across the table and put her hand over Tina's.

"Every family has issues," Lisa declared. "I don't know anybody who isn't screwed up. Look at me."

Tina and Clara suddenly burst out laughing, and Lisa giggled.

"That journalist said I could be an inspiration for girls," Tina said. "Maybe we should consider…"

"No!" Clara said sharply. "Our family has to remain anonymous. It's about Christmas, not us." She sighed heavily. "And let's not tell your father about this."

11 *Surprise Guest*

"I can't believe that we're about to do this." Tina gripped George's hand tightly as the plane neared Boston.

"Just a few more days and nothing will separate us." George squeezed her hand.

"Except for time and distance," she said ruefully.

"We'll be united in spirit. I'm glad we're making this commitment. Now I feel like I won't lose you."

"How could you think you'd ever lose me?" Tina asked with surprise.

"You did have your old boyfriend, Kai, hanging around you at the North Pole," George reminded her. "For all I know, he's still up there plotting to steal you away from me."

"I hope you're kidding," Tina replied. "I'm not interested in him and he has a girlfriend, anyway."

"I know. I trust you."

"And how do I know you don't have a groupie in every city?" Tina asked, remembering Courtney's remarks.

"I do, but you'll be my main one," he teased.

"Seriously, George, Courtney was talking about it last week, and it made me a little nervous," she admitted.

"Don't listen to her. You know I don't want anybody but you, and I'll be crying into my pillow every night we're apart." He gave Tina a kiss.

"Okay. Quit being cute, you two," Lisa said from the seat behind them.

"Leave them alone," Walter chided. "They're happy."

"Oh, my gosh. I'm surrounded by saps," she exclaimed.

Loren tapped her on the shoulder. "Hey, I'm with you. I know they're getting married, but I don't know how much more my stomach can take."

Walter scowled and pulled Lisa closer to him. He

knew that they'd had a serious flirtation last year during his brief separation from her. He agreed with Nick that Loren was trouble and felt uncomfortable whenever Loren was around Lisa.

"Oh, Walter, I didn't see you there." Loren chuckled.

"Ignore him," Lisa said loudly enough for him to hear. "Loren, don't be a jerk."

"I'm really looking forward to meeting your parents, George," Clara leaned into the aisle to say. "Right, dear?" She prodded Santa.

"Hmm?" He roused from his nap.

"I think we should've eloped," George whispered to Tina, and she giggled.

"I hope my dress doesn't get wrinkled," Courtney stated. "Did I pack my steamer?"

"I don't know," John responded. "And I don't get why you packed so much. We're only going to be there a few days."

"I have a steamer," Tina called back to her.

"Tina brought everything but the kitchen sink," Lisa remarked.

"I had to pack for the honeymoon. We're going straight to Hawaii after this," Tina said. "And then I'm flying home. I had to pack clothes for warm weather and clothes for cold weather and everything I have to bring home."

"Kris, did you remember my good shirt?" Nick asked.

"Yup. I packed all the stuff on your list," Kris answered.

"Nick, did you make Kris pack for you?" Clara turned in her seat. "I told you not to take advantage of your cousin."

"Mom, he's my personal assistant when we're not on tour," Nick said. "He's cool with it."

"Yeah," Kris said. "I don't mind."

Clara shook her head. She spoke in a hushed tone to Santa. "Isn't it nice that nobody recognizes you since you shaved and lost weight? People used to ask you all the time if you were him."

"I don't know how we're going to handle an outsider in the family," Santa grumbled.

"Don't worry." Clara patted his arm. "The most important thing is that our daughter is happy."

"It was so nice of Robin to charter this plane for us," Tina said.

"It's too bad he couldn't make the wedding," George said.

Tina sighed. "Every time I turn around, I'm on a plane."

"Too bad you can't get the reindeer to fly you around," George whispered.

"The union contract wouldn't allow it. Besides, they like their time off," Tina informed him.

"I was kidding."

"Oh." She smiled. "You know, it's weird that I haven't heard from that journalist again. She said she was going to call me again in a few days, but she hasn't."

"Maybe she gave up," George guessed.

"I hope so. I have enough on my mind. I still haven't figured out how to handle it, anyway."

Tina looked out the window at the clouds. This was becoming a familiar sight.

***

Tina stood in front of the full-length mirror in Gemma's bedroom. The lacy dress draped over her body perfectly. The front hem was shorter, and the back hem brushed against her lace-covered heels. A round headpiece held a veil that trailed to her shoulder blades. Gemma had fixed her hair, and ringlets fell about her face with the rest of her hair in a tousled pile on top of her head. Courtney had done her makeup, though she'd had to wipe some of it off. Tina was transfixed by her own image and felt like she was in a dream.

"She looks lovely," Gloria said to Clara.

Gemma played with a ringlet on the right side of her face. "There."

"I think you need a little more eye shadow." Courtney approached, but Tina waved her away.

"She looks perfect," Lisa said. She stepped closer to Tina. "This is it. You're a vision and he's going to cry when he sees you."

Tina studied Lisa in the mirror. "Look at you. That pale blue looks beautiful on you, maid-of-honor. Soon it will be your turn."

"One wedding at a time." Lisa smiled.

"How's Walter?" Tina asked.

"He's fine. He's sitting with Nick. George's family has been very nice to him."

"Good." Tina stared at herself in the mirror.

"How are we going to cover her face with the veil without messing up her hair?" Gloria asked Gemma.

Tina turned to look at them. "I don't want my face covered. I want to see everything clearly."

Clara dabbed her eyes with a tissue. "I'm going to be a mess by the end of the day."

Gloria put her arm around Clara's shoulder. "I'm sure I'll start crying as soon as I see George."

Gemma hugged Tina. "Welcome to the family, sister."

Tina turned to Courtney. "Ready to take pictures?"

"I already took a bunch and John is in the hall with your father with the video camera." Courtney nodded at her. "You go, girl, and show me how it's done."

Tina ignored the butterfly frenzy in her stomach and looked at the clock on the wall.

Lisa followed her gaze. "It's time."

Oh, why hadn't they eloped? This was the most nerve-wracking thing Tina had ever done. She glanced around at the other women. She was glad to share this day with their families and friends, but she couldn't wait for the ceremony to be over. Perhaps then her stomach would finally settle. She placed her hand on her tummy.

"You're not..." Courtney noticed her hand.

"No, of course not," Tina responded quickly. "I just have butterflies."

Lisa shot Courtney an annoyed look and turned back to Tina. "Let's go, bestie, before I cry like a water fountain."

Tina opened the door and saw her father. She'd never seen him in a suit. His hair was neatly combed, and he looked trim and dapper. He seemed uncomfortable, and she smiled at him with affection. His mouth dropped open a little when he saw her, but he recovered and cleared his throat.

"You look very nice, Tina."

"Thanks, Dad. You too." She stepped forward and linked her arm in his.

"When did you grow up?" He shook his head.

Lisa rushed ahead and leaned over the banister. "Start the music. They're coming."

Tina heard the CD play the opening notes of the traditional wedding march. For a moment, her knees felt weak.

"I got you," Santa said.

Tina felt numb as she watched their mothers and Gemma hurry downstairs to take their seats. Courtney ran down the steps ahead of them and took more photos as Lisa descended the stairs to Nick, who waited for her. They paused at the entrance to the living room and Tina saw George. He was dressed in a navy suit with a pale blue tie, and his hair was neatly pulled back into a ponytail. His smile was wide, and she couldn't wait to get to him.

They slowly stepped toward the minister. Tina was glad John was recording the ceremony because it was all a blur until she heard the words, "I now pronounce you husband and wife."

They turned to each other. "We did it," George murmured. "We're married."

He kissed her, and she felt dizzy. One second they were standing there and the next they were magically married. It was surreal.

George took Tina's hand. "You're shaking."

Clara rushed over and grabbed her into a suffocating embrace. "Congratulations, sweetie." Then she hugged George.

Lisa hugged her. Her father hugged her. Walter hugged her. Nick hugged her. George's parents hugged her. Gemma hugged her. G.G. hugged her. Garrett, Tonia, and Evan hugged her. Everyone hugged them. Tina felt great relief as the stress seeped from her body. Now she could relax and enjoy the reception. And then... her butterflies surged again... the honeymoon.

Her father's brother, Kris Kringle, and his wife were in attendance. Aunt Kandi's white hair was gathered in a bun at the nape of her neck. She looked elegant, though she wore too much makeup. Tina was glad that her father and uncle had mended their differences. This was the first time they'd seen each other in years, and she was glad to give them this auspicious occasion to reconnect.

Tina noticed Kris hardly spoke to his parents, preferring to stick by Nick's side, but she decided not to worry about anything today. It was difficult enough trying to remember the names of George's extended family and his parents' friends. There were more people than they'd intended to include in their small wedding. But it didn't matter. She and George were married and nothing was going to bother her today.

"Tina, have you seen Nick?" Kris asked anxiously.

She looked around. "I'm sure he's around here somewhere."

She noticed her stomach was growling and headed toward the buffet table. George was talking with his father and she started toward them.

"Tina? Congratulations."

A youngish woman extended her hand. She had dark shoulder-length hair and wore tortoiseshell glasses. She held a plastic cup in one hand and had a large purse slung over her shoulder.

"Yes, thank you for coming. Are you related to George?" Tina asked pleasantly, taking the woman's hand.

"Oh, hey," Kris said to the woman.

"Hello, Kris." She turned back to Tina, still grasping her hand. "We haven't met, though we've spoken on the phone. I'm Jill Graham from..."

Tina gasped and pulled her hand away. She glanced around to see if she'd drawn anyone's attention and turned to Kris. "You know her?"

"Yeah, I invited her. She said she wanted to meet you." He shrugged.

Tina yanked his arm to bring him closer to her. "What have you done?" she demanded in a low voice. "Why didn't you ask me before you invited her?"

"Hey," Kris protested. "That hurts."

"Don't tell anyone she's here, Kris."

Tina motioned for Jill to follow her. They went into the hall and Tina quickly looked around for somewhere they could speak privately. The bathroom door was ajar, so they entered and closed the door.

"I'm sorry to crash your wedding." Jill set her cup on the bathroom counter. "Kris invited me and didn't think you'd mind."

"Kris is your source?" Tina asked incredulously. "I can't believe this." She paced within their confined space.

Jill stared at her. "Your hair. It's all white. I don't know what I expected, but you've exceeded my expectations. That doesn't sound like it makes sense, but..." She shook her head. "You look stunning. I was trying to figure out who your father is. Is he the one with the white beard and mustache?"

"That's my uncle." Tina stopped and stared at Jill. "I appreciate that you're trying to do your job, but this is my wedding day..."

"Does your husband know who you are?"

This was the first time that someone had referred to George as her husband. Tina let the words sink in. It sounded nice.

"No, I mean, yes. Of course, he knows who I am, but his family doesn't. Most of the people here don't know who we are, and I want to keep it that way." Tina closed the toilet and sat on the seat. She put her head in her hands and moaned. "We've remained anonymous for generations, and my parents want to continue that tradition. I'm sorry. I can't give you an interview."

Jill sat down on the edge of the tub. "I understand. I shouldn't have intruded."

"I think you're right that it *would* be an inspiration for girls," Tina conceded. "But it's not only about me. My family wants to stay anonymous. My mother said it's about Christmas, not us, and I agree with her. I don't want to become a celebrity."

"Unlike your brother," Jill said.

"That's different. He's not trying to cash in on our name. It's all about his band," Tina responded. "You should interview him. Not as a Claus, but as a rock star. He'd love it. It would be good publicity for the band. All the band members are all here today."

Jill shook her head. "I don't think that would work for the magazine." She reached over for her cup and took a sip. "After I did the article about Princess Ava, the Royal Charitable Trust was inundated with donations."

"That's great."

"My point is that there was an unexpected benefit from the publicity."

"Well, we don't need donations and we don't want publicity," Tina stated. "It's not..."

There was a knock on the door. "Tina, are you

okay?" Lisa asked in a hushed tone.

Tina got up and let Lisa in. "This is Jill, the journalist who's been calling us."

"What are you doing here?" Lisa stared at Jill, aghast.

"It was Kris," Tina said. "He's the source."

"Why am I not surprised?" Lisa said sarcastically. "So, what's happening here?"

"I was telling Jill that not everyone here knows who we are," Tina filled her in. "We were just…"

There was another knock on the door. "Tina, it's me," George said. "I just wanted to make sure you're okay."

Lisa opened the door, and he stepped into the crowded bathroom. "What's going on? Is everything okay?"

"Meet Jill." Lisa waved at her. "She's that journalist."

"Congratulations," Jill said to him, unperturbed.

"Thanks." He looked at Tina with confusion. "Are you giving her an interview in the bathroom?"

"No, I was explaining to her why I *can't* give her an interview," Tina responded. She turned back to Jill. "I'm sorry if you came a long way, but Kris doesn't speak for me or the family. I'd really appreciate your discretion."

Jill stood. "I guess I'm leaving." She set her cup down. "It was nice to meet you. I wish you the best." She pulled a business card out of her purse and set it on the bathroom counter. "I hope you change your mind. Please think about it. Think about the little girls." She smiled as she brushed past them to the door.

Tina waited until the door had closed behind her. "It was Kris! I should've known." She picked up the card and handed it to George. "Can you put this in your pocket?"

"We should probably get out of here in case someone wants to use the bathroom," George said.

They spilled out into the hallway. Gloria was

outside the door and looked up in surprise.

"Is something wrong?" she asked.

"Just a little meeting," Lisa said breezily.

"Everything's fine, Mom," George assured her.

"I have to find Kris," Tina told Lisa.

She scanned the living room and saw him in the dining room by the food. He was stuffing a deviled egg into his mouth. She contemplated what to say to him without making a scene.

"Oh, no," Lisa said.

"What?"

"It looks like Loren is flirting with Gemma. Do you believe him? Can't he give it a rest for one day?"

"I'm sure she can handle herself," Tina said and hurried toward Kris. She took his arm and pulled him over into the corner by the window.

"Hey, Tina," Kris said. "Where's Jill?"

"Kris, why did you tell Jill who we are?" she fumed. "Nobody is supposed to know."

"Nick said something about that, too." He furrowed his brow. "What's the big deal, anyway? Publicity is good."

Tina took a deep breath. "I know you've never been away from home before, but didn't your parents tell you that you can't tell anyone who we are outside of the Pole?"

"Um..." He squinted. "I don't know. They might've mentioned it."

"Okay, listen to me," Tina said adamantly. "Don't tell anyone who doesn't already know. Nobody in the band except George. Nobody else. Got it?"

"But I thought it'd be good publicity for the band. Nick is always saying we need press," Kris said defensively. "Anyway, she's the one who started talking to me at one of the gigs. I didn't know it was a big secret. Geez." He yanked his arm away.

Tina shook her head. "Okay. Just promise me you won't tell anyone else. Okay?"

"Yeah," Kris answered sullenly. "Whatever."

12 *Hot and Cold*

"*This* is what I've been looking forward to," George said, taking Tina's hand. "Being alone with you."

She smiled fondly at him and tilted her face upwards for a moment. "The sun feels so good." She brushed a bit of sand off her towel. "I've never seen black sand before."

"It's from the lava."

"I can't wait to go to Volcano Park tomorrow," she enthused. "But I just want to relax today."

"Yeah. The wedding got out of control. My parents invited too many people..."

"And then Jill showed up. Why would Kris invite her to our wedding? I was so angry at him."

"I don't blame you," George said. "Then we had that long flight yesterday, but even though we were exhausted, we still had our honeymoon night."

Tina smiled and blushed. "I don't even remember most of the wedding. I can't wait to see the video."

"Yeah. I hope John got most of the guests on the video. I never realized my parents had so many friends and obscure relatives."

"Where did you put Jill's business card?"

"I stuck it in your purse. Why?"

"Just wondering."

"Did you see all those gifts? We got some nice things. I just have to find a condo to put it all in. I'll start looking again as soon as I get back. Then we'll have a place that's all ours." He leaned over and kissed her shoulder.

"We have a ton of thank-you cards to write." Tina sighed. "I asked Lisa to make a list of everything and who it's from, and then I'll work on that when I get back home. I guess we'll have two homes."

"Anywhere you are is home to me," George said.

"I guess my parents' apartment at the Pole is mine now that they're retired and live in Florida." Tina shrugged. "Maybe I'll redecorate a little."

"I never thought in my wildest dreams I'd be married to the new Santa." George grinned.

Tina smiled. "I never thought I'd be married to my brother's best friend."

"Wife."

"Husband."

They blissfully cuddled on the towel and gazed out at the pale blue water washing up onto the black sand while palm trees rustled above in the gentle breeze. This was a perfect moment.

Tina didn't want to think about anything else. Not work. Not journalists. And she especially didn't want to think about having to part from George. Reality would intrude soon enough.

***

Nick had a plan. It might be a little evil, but Loren had started this war. Despite George's absence, the band must go on and they had new songs to rehearse. He'd get George up to speed later. Once he returned from his honeymoon, everything would be back on track.

Nick had written another song that he and Isabella could perform together during their next tour. He knew if he kept coming up with songs, they'd have to keep rehearsing together and that would give him more opportunities to be close to her, though he preferred writing songs *with* her because that meant even more time alone. But he didn't want to push it. She had to come to him. His ego demanded it. Luckily, *Black Ice* was opening for *Rock Goddess* again. Time on the road would throw them together and, at some point, she'd realize how she felt about him. It was inevitable.

But right now, he needed to discern how to disrupt Loren's bond with Isabella. Loren wasn't serious about her. He wasn't serious about anybody. Yet they stood in an intimate huddle talking, and it irked Nick. He was going to put a stop to this. Loren was only doing it to get to him, and Isabella was just trying to make him jealous. He was sure of it.

John lingered by the drums talking to Milo who tapped his drums impatiently. Then, to Nick's dismay, he disrupted Loren and Isabella's intimacy for him.

"Hey, Loren," Milo called. "Did I see you hitting on George's sister at the wedding?" He let out a guffaw and hit the cymbals.

Loren looked up with surprise and quickly recovered. "Why? Are you jealous?" he responded. "I got her number."

"And she probably has yours," John retorted. He and Milo laughed.

Isabella turned with a slight smile and took her place in front of her mic. She glanced over at Lilliana and then said over her shoulder.

"Hey, Nick. What are you doing later?"

"Uh..."

"Good. After rehearsal then."

Kris punched his shoulder. "You and Isabella. That's what you..."

"Kris." Nick glared at him. Kris had such a big mouth. "Tina wanted me to talk to you."

"What about? That reporter?"

"What reporter?" John asked. "Are you doing an interview?"

"No, it's about Tina." Nick was even more irritated with Kris. "Let's go upstairs and get some beers. We'll be right back, guys."

Kris followed him up the steps from the basement and into Milo's kitchen.

"Kris." Nick shook his head in exasperation. "What's wrong with you? Discretion, man. Never talk about our family and be cool about Isabella."

"What's the problem? I thought you said we needed more PR."

"We do. For the band. Not for the family business." Nick grimaced. "Just don't mention our family to anyone. Don't mention the North Pole. Don't even mention Christmas."

"All right. All right." Kris held up his hands in surrender.

"And as far as Isabella is concerned," Nick said. "It's delicate. Don't blow it for me. Don't say anything that anyone can hear. Got it?"

"Geez. Whatever, dude."

Nick took a beer. "Grab that six-pack and bring it downstairs."

Kris obediently retrieved it from the refrigerator. "Are you mad at me?" he asked forlornly.

Nick sighed heavily. "I know you didn't do it on purpose. Just think about what you say, okay?"

"Yeah. I can do that." Kris followed him back down the stairs.

***

"It's good to be home," Walter said. "I know there isn't much room in the closet, but we'll shift things around so they work better. I want you to be comfortable here."

Lisa perched on the small couch. "I feel so big when I'm here. I guess I'll get used to it."

"I'm sorry it's not as spacious as the apartment."

"We could spend some time over there," she suggested hopefully.

"I don't think we should. It's Tina and George's place now."

"I guess you're right, but I didn't move all of my stuff out yet. Not that I have a lot, but I didn't know where to put it."

Walter sat next to her and took her hand. "It's always an adjustment to move in with someone. I know you're making all the sacrifices and I appreciate it. We'll work it out and find room for all your stuff."

"Thanks, Walter. I feel a little freaked out." Lisa gave him a weak smile. "It's even scarier because I know I can't go back to the apartment now that Tina and George are married."

"This is your home now, Lisa."

"I know, but what if we have a big fight? I'd have nowhere to go. I'd be homeless," she fretted.

"I'm sure there's plenty of room in the barn with the reindeer," he joked.

"That's not funny." Lisa pulled her hand away.

"I'm sorry." Walter took her hand again. "I'd never throw you out, and Tina would never throw you out either. Besides, George won't be here most of the time."

"That's true." She perked up. "That makes me feel better. I guess I need to feel like I have a safety net just in case."

"You'll never have to use it," Walter assured her. "We got along great during our vacation and you know how I feel about you."

"I know. I'm probably being ridiculous. I should be happy to be here with you, and I am. I really am."

"Well, it's nice to be home, especially since you're here now." He smiled at her with affection. "But I always dread going into the office on the first day back because there are so many emails and messages."

"You're not going in tomorrow, are you?"

"No, not for a few days. At least it's nice and quiet until everybody else gets back," Walter said. "We're getting a late start because of the wedding, but it'll be fine."

"Wasn't the wedding great? And Tina looked beautiful."

"Yes, she did, and so did you," Walter said. "Tina and George looked so happy and George's family is nice. I talked to his grandmother for a long time."

"She was great. It's too bad that journalist showed up."

"You don't think she'll bother Tina anymore, do you?" he asked.

"Tina made it pretty clear that she wasn't doing an interview, and she seemed to accept it. I just don't understand why Kris would've invited her. What was he thinking?"

"Kris grew up pretty sheltered, and I don't think he realized how different it would be outside of the North Pole," Walter said. "I don't think he gives things much thought."

"That's an understatement."

They both laughed.

"I'm glad Nick hired him to work for the band, though. He's such a huge fan, and it was a good solution." Walter sank back onto the couch. "Are you hungry? We could go out or just open up a few cans of soup. Maybe there's a movie on TV."

"I don't feel like getting all bundled up to go out," Lisa said. "Soup sounds good to me. What is it with soup around here?"

"Canned soup keeps for a long time. You can stock up on it. Besides, soup is perfect when it's cold outside and it's always cold outside here."

"Sold," Lisa said.

Walter stood up. "I should probably go out to the main barn to see the reindeer tomorrow. I always let them know when I'm back and I can tell them how the wedding went."

"Can I go too?" Lisa asked eagerly. "I've only seen them at the pub or on Christmas Eve when they're hooked up to the sleigh."

"I don't know if I should bring you out there," Walter said with hesitation. "You know how they are. They can be intimidating, and they don't like visitors. I even get nervous when I have to go out there. They're not the friendliest bunch."

"Oh, they can't be that bad. They raise a ruckus at the pub, but they're just having fun." Lisa waved her hand dismissively.

Walter considered it. "I don't know. Let's talk about it tomorrow." But he didn't feel comfortable with the idea.

***

Isabella pushed aside the beer that Nick offered her. "We've been rehearsing for hours. Let's go get a real drink."

She glanced in Loren's direction as she sidled up to Nick and brushed her fingertips gently along his cheek. He was momentarily frozen.

"Uh... right. Great rehearsal, guys. Let's call it a day," Nick said quickly.

Everyone mumbled their agreement and packed up their equipment.

"Talk to you later, Is," Lilliana said, unstrapping her guitar and placing it in the case.

Nick followed Isabella up the stairs, not sure what to expect. Was she finally coming to her senses?

"Okay." She put a hand out to stop him when they reached the top. "Let's just get something to eat. I've had nothing but a smoothie all day."

"Right."

"We can take your car. I came with Lill."

She turned, and he followed her to the front door. She slipped on her sandals and they stepped outside into the cool of early evening.

"There aren't many places I can go where I don't get mobbed by fans. Pretty soon you'll have that problem too," she said when they got in the car.

"I'm working on it."

Isabella shook her head. "It's not a problem you want to have. It's terrible not being able to go wherever you want. At first, it was exciting, and it still is, but not having any privacy sucks."

Nick started the car.

"Head into the city," she said. "All the love I get from fans when I'm onstage is the best, but I just want to relax and be myself when I'm offstage, you know?"

"Where do you want to go?"

"I'll direct you," she said. "Fame is a lot of pressure. Enjoy being unknown while you still can."

Nick could feel Isabella studying him. It made him anxious. He finally had her all to himself, and he wasn't sure what to do with her. She muddled his mind. She was hot and cold, just like most women. He tried to think of something smart and clever to say.

"Turn right and then turn left at the next light." She settled back in her seat.

"Do you like Loren?" Had he said that out loud? Why had he brought up Loren? He mentally kicked himself.

She giggled. "I knew you were jealous."

"No way," he blurted.

Nick kept his mouth shut until they got to the restaurant. She was silent as well, except to give him directions. They soon arrived at an upscale restaurant with a crowded parking lot.

"There's valet service here. Just pull up," Isabella instructed. "They know me here." She jumped out of the car. "They'll give us a private booth."

Nick trailed behind her flowing skirt until they were inside. Her graceful movements never failed to mesmerize him. They followed the hostess upstairs to a private area and were seated in a dark, cozy booth.

"I'm starving," she announced as she perused the menu.

They ordered fancy drinks and Nick picked up his menu. Everything was expensive. It gave him a twinge of excitement to think that he was now successful enough to be here dining with Isabella. He could afford overpriced meals now, but wait a minute. Was he selling out? He looked around and his eyes fell on her face, glowing in the candlelight. His mind went blank. What had he been thinking about a minute ago?

After they ordered, Isabella leaned back and stared at him. "You impress me, Nick. You're so prolific. I wish I could write as many songs as you."

"Right."

She leaned forward when their drinks arrived. "Thanks," she said to the server and ordered meals for both of them. She took a sip of her drink. "Mmm. I needed this." She took another long sip. "But I mean it. I'm impressed. You really are talented, you know."

"Right. I'm a big fan of you... yours."

Her laugh was light and floated around them. "The fans like our collaborations." She tilted her head. "You know what would get us both some good PR? I know Robin would love this idea."

"What?" What would their mutual manager love?

"If people thought we were collaborating offstage as well." She smiled coyly.

"We do. We write..."

"That's not what I mean, Nicky." She slid closer to him in the booth. "You know I don't get involved with other musicians, but we can pretend. The fans would love it."

"Right." Nick wasn't sure what she was proposing.

"We just have to be seen out together and let people speculate." She pulled her drink over and took another long sip. "This drink is pure ambrosia. Food of the gods. And goddesses." She laughed mellifluously.

Nick gulped his drink. His addlepated mind tried to sort out the implications of her suggestion. What exactly was she suggesting, anyway?

"What do you think, Nicky? Can you handle a goddess?" Isabella smiled.

13 *Game Within a Game*

"Did you speak with your brother at the wedding?" Clara asked Santa.

"What is there to eat?" He peered toward the kitchen.

"Is that all you can think about? We're going out to eat with Myra and Marty tonight, remember?" she answered. "Did you speak with your brother?"

"What kind of question is that? Of course, I spoke to my brother. We're on speaking terms again."

"I mean, did you speak to him about his son? Kris has to realize that we have to be discreet when we're not at the North Pole. Did you tell him that his son spoke to a reporter?" she demanded.

"Yes, I had a word with him. I don't think much damage was done."

"I certainly hope not. Tina said she hasn't heard from that reporter since the wedding." Clara sat on the couch. "Kandi looked lovely, didn't she? It was very nice of them to come all that way to our daughter's wedding. I'm glad that you and your brother have patched things up."

"Our little girl is married," Santa said wistfully, shaking his head.

"We couldn't have picked a better son-in-law, other than his family isn't from the North Pole," Clara said. "Do you think we'll eventually have to tell them? That's just too many people."

"Hmm." Santa stroked his chin. He was still getting used to being clean-shaven. "I always thought Tina would marry Kai."

"I did too, but he ran off after they graduated high school."

"George is a fine young man."

"Yes, and Gloria and Grover are wonderful people. Their little grandson, Evan, was adorable. He was attached to you like glue."

"Children know." Santa nodded. "They sense who I am."

"One of these days, we'll have our own grandchildren. I can't wait." Clara's smile changed into a frown. "Will Tina be able to ride the sleigh when she's pregnant?"

"Good question. It's never been done."

"Our daughter is breaking all kinds of barriers. Now, aren't you proud of her?"

"What kind of question is that? Of course, I am."

"I wish George's family was closer. Wouldn't it be nice to get to know them better? We're family now. We're all so spread out," she lamented.

"Hmm."

"Do you think Nick will ever settle down?" Clara wondered.

"Nick? Who would be crazy enough to marry Nick? He could drive a saint to drink."

"Now stop that. You're talking about our son, dear," she scolded. "I know you two butt heads, but it's only because he wanted to do his own thing."

"He doesn't respect our name and what we stand for," Santa grumbled. "I don't know where we went wrong with that one."

"There's nothing wrong with Nick. He's just…"

"He and Kris make a fine pair… of dimwits." He chuckled.

"Dear, stop talking about our son that way. Nick is very intelligent… in certain ways. He's creative, artistic. He just… you two just don't communicate well." Clara shook her head. "But Tina has come through for us. I just hope that reporter… What was her name? Wait a minute. I have Myra's magazine right here." She picked it up from the end table. "Let's see."

"An interview is out of the question," Santa asserted.

"Tina is well aware of that."

"You can't tell people. They have to believe on their

own. Just like children do," Santa intoned. "They have pure spirits and open hearts."

Clara looked up from the magazine. "You miss it, don't you?"

Santa shrugged.

"We'll go up there and help at the end of the season. I'm curious to see the changes Tina has made. I'm sure we'll be very impressed and you'll feel better about handing it over to her." Clara got up and went over to Santa in his recliner. "I'm glad you retired before you worked yourself to death, dear." She rubbed his back reassuringly.

"Sometimes I don't know what to do with myself," Santa admitted.

"I know." Clara put her arms around him. "Let's enjoy our retirement. Myra was talking about the four of us going on a cruise. That sounds fun, doesn't it?"

"A cruise?" he barked. "I've been all over the world. What do I want with a cruise?"

"I haven't been all over the world. I think a cruise sounds nice." Clara patted his arm. "Let's think about it."

***

"Now remember what I told you," Walter said as they trudged along the path to the main barn.

"Yeah, I know. Blitzen thinks he's the boss and Rudolph likes attention," Lisa said.

"Blitzen likes to intimidate people," he reminded her. "The reindeer are huge, so it's easy to feel scared. Just don't say anything and you'll be fine."

"I told you. I've seen them at the pub. They're not that scary."

"Okay." Walter sighed and his breath came out in a frosty cloud.

She'd find out soon enough, and then she wouldn't be so quick to go out to the main barn anymore.

"Oi," Donner called to them from the doorway of the barn. "Is that you, Walter? And who do we have here?"

"Yes, it's me," Walter answered. "This is Lisa. She's Tina's assistant and also my girlfriend."

"A bit of a soap opera, have we?" He nodded. "Come inside before you freeze to death."

They stepped into the barn and stamped the snow off their feet. Lisa scanned the cavernous interior. There was a wood stove in the corner, but no other reindeer to be seen.

"Who's here?" Rudolph came bounding out from an opening at the back.

"Hi, Rudy," Walter said. "This is Lisa..."

"Tina's assistant and Walter's girlfriend," Donner finished.

"I've seen you doing karaoke," Lisa told him. "You're pretty good."

"You think so?" Rudolph asked happily.

The rest of the reindeer wandered out at the sound of their voices, and Walter greeted them and introduced Lisa. She was delighted to meet them. Up close, they were magnificent animals.

"I'm thrilled to finally meet you," Lisa said humbly. "You're... you're legends."

"Ah, now isn't she cute?" Prancer said.

"I love the color of your hair." Dancer circled her. "What would you call that? Tawny?"

"Are you two an item?" Vixen asked. "Good for you, Walter. It was time for you to move on."

Lisa noticed the largest reindeer eyeing her suspiciously.

"You must be Blitzen," she said to him. "I'm honored to meet you, sir."

He shook his heavy head. "Well, thank you, young lady. No need to call me sir."

Walter cleared his throat. "I just wanted to let you know that we're back."

"How was the wedding?" Dasher asked. "I bet it was

lovely."

"We're so happy for Tina," Cupid said. "I remember when she was just a little girl. They grow so fast."

"That's so true." Prancer nodded.

"I wish you could've seen her. She was stunning," Lisa said. "She wore this old-fashioned lacy dress and you should've seen George's face when he saw her coming down the aisle toward him."

"How romantic." Vixen sighed.

"We took a video," Lisa said.

"I want to see it," Dancer said eagerly.

"We don't have it yet," Walter answered.

"Tina might have a copy," Lisa said.

"We can have a screening," Dancer suggested. "It'll be fun."

"Tell Tina to bring it out here so we can see it when she gets back," Blitzen ordered.

"Okay," Lisa said.

He clopped closer and stood towering over them. Lisa stared up at him in wonder. His breath came out in a cloud of mist, and the many branches of his antlers reached upward. He seemed majestic and powerful. She was in awe.

Walter cleared his throat. "Tina should be back soon. We're a little behind schedule because of the wedding."

"The mailroom will be busy. We picked up tons of mail from the post office. It looks like we got quite a bit more than last year," Blitzen reported. "They had trouble storing it all."

"Okay. Maybe we can pay them to deliver it again while you're on vacation next season like we used to, so it doesn't pile up at the post office," Walter said thoughtfully. "I'll talk to Tina about it. It shouldn't be a problem."

"Good. I also want to bring up an issue with the sleigh," Blitzen remembered, turning his massive head toward Walter.

"What is it? I'll see what I can do," Walter said.

"The big sleigh needs servicing. There was a little drag on the runners last year and the harnesses are getting frayed," Blitzen informed him. "It's in our contract that these things have to be maintained. I don't have to tell you, Walter, how uncomfortable the harnesses are when they're frayed."

"Don't worry, Blitzen. Tina has regular servicing scheduled for all the sleighs. There will be yearly maintenance on the smaller postal sleighs because they get used more often, and we'll have the big sleigh checked at the same time," Walter promised. "I think it's scheduled soon after she returns so she can approve any repairs."

Blitzen nodded. "Sounds like she's got it covered. Tina's always on top of things. Guess I can't complain."

Walter had never heard Blitzen say that in all his years on the job.

"You two better get back. It's too cold out here for you," Dasher advised, pushing them toward the door.

"Remember to bring the wedding video out for us," Dancer called after them.

"I don't know why everyone is afraid of the reindeer," Lisa said as they hurried along the path. "They were perfectly nice to me."

***

Tina lugged the suitcases into her bedroom at the North Pole and unpacked. Then she peeked into the closet in one of the other bedrooms. Most of Lisa's clothes were gone. Tina meandered out to the living room and sat on the couch in silence. She missed George. There was an empty ache in the middle of her chest that had settled there after they'd parted. And now Lisa was gone too. It would've been easier if she were still there to commiserate with.

Suddenly, the door swung open, and Lisa burst into

the room carrying a grocery bag.

"I was hoping to beat you here. I turned up the heat yesterday and picked up some food for you when Walter and I went shopping."

Lisa hung up her coat and kicked off her boots.

"I'm so happy to see you!" Tina cried. "Thank you!"

Lisa smiled. "We have a lot of catching up to do. I told Walter I was staying over here tonight. I think it's good for couples to spend a little time apart. Otherwise, they can drive each other crazy."

"Is Walter driving you crazy?" Tina asked with concern.

"I'm not used to being with someone all the time," Lisa said. "It freaks me out a little. I mean, I love Walter. I enjoy being with him, but you know me. I freak out if I'm too happy."

Tina laughed. "You're so weird."

"But in a good way, right?" Lisa grinned.

"Yes. I don't know what I'd do without you."

Tina was thankful to have such a good friend and ran over to hug her.

"You're probably hungry. I made a casserole from one of your mother's recipes. I'll just pop it in the oven." Lisa headed toward the kitchen.

"That sounds great."

Tina flipped the switch for the gas fireplace and watched the flames shoot up between the ceramic logs as Lisa disappeared into the kitchen and began putting away the groceries.

"Okay. It shouldn't take too long to warm up." Lisa crossed the room, and they settled onto the couch. Lisa nudged Tina.

"Sooo, how was the honeymoon?"

"Oh." Tina blushed. "It was perfect. George is so romantic and wonderful. I have a lot of pictures to show you. We drove all over the island..." Her voice trailed off.

"I know. It's hard to be apart." Lisa nodded sympathetically.

"How was *your* vacation? We didn't get to talk much at the wedding. So much was going on. Do you have any pictures?"

"Yeah. We can do the picture thing in a while. I think I'm going to make some hot chocolate. Do you want some? It'll warm us up."

"Okay."

Lisa went back into the kitchen. Tina could see over the counter while Lisa peeked into the oven.

"Oh! I forgot to tell you." She whirled to look at Tina. "I met the reindeer when we first got back."

"You went out to the barn?" Tina asked with disbelief.

"Yeah, Walter was reluctant to bring me out there, but I really wanted to meet them, even though I've seen them at the pub."

"I hope Blitzen was nice. He doesn't like strangers."

"He was fine." Lisa waved her hand. "He said something about maintenance for the sleighs."

"Oh, yes. I have that scheduled," Tina remembered.

"It was so cool to see them up close," Lisa said, wide-eyed with excitement. "It was incredible. I still can't believe I'm here at the North Pole. How crazy is that?" She giggled.

Tina smiled at her exuberance. Then she stifled a yawn. Her stomach was growling, and she was probably dehydrated.

"I have so much to do. I probably have a million voicemails and emails. It'll take a while to get caught up."

"Walter took care of a lot of them," Lisa assured her. "Oh, Blitzen said there's a ton of mail."

"He probably means that literally."

"Don't worry. I'll help you. We'll catch up once the elves return to work. We just have to get back into the swing of things."

"Thanks for coming over tonight," Tina said. "I was feeling lonely. I don't know how I'm going to get through the next few months without George.”

“Well, even though you went and got married and I lost my mind and moved in with Walter, I’ve still got your back,” Lisa said. “Now I want to hear all about Hawaii and your perfect honeymoon and see those pictures.”

***

“Nicky, look at me,” Isabella instructed.

She ran her fingertips along his cheek. Then she gave him a light kiss on the lips just as a bright flash blinded him. He blinked as white spots danced around the edges of his vision and her kiss tantalizingly lingered on his lips.

“Good. They got the picture,” she whispered. “Remember, we’re going to deny everything and let them assume.”

Nick took a sip of the fancy drink she’d ordered for him in this trendy club. She was pressed against him, and it made him a little dizzy to be so close to her. He struggled to think clearly. Why did she make his thoughts so fuzzy?

“Want to dance?” she asked.

There was no way he was going to twitch around a dance floor and look like a fool.

“I don’t dance.” He scowled.

“You dance on stage.”

“That’s not dancing. That’s performing.”

Nick tried to recall. Did he really move around that much onstage?

“Same thing.” Isabella sipped her drink. “I like to dance. I like to let the music move me.” She swayed on her barstool.

He chugged the rest of his drink and shakily stood. “Let’s get out of here.”

“Why? I’m having fun.” She pouted and stood directly in front of him. “Why do you want to leave,

Nicky?" she murmured.

He stared into her eyes, unable to speak.

"You're right," she blurted. "Let them speculate about where we're going." She downed her drink and took his hand. "Let's get out of here," she said in a loud voice.

Nick let Isabella pull him through the club until they pushed through the doors to the outside. The night air was cool, and he realized how warm and claustrophobic it had been inside. The valet retrieved his car, and they hopped in as another flashbulb popped.

"That was fun," she said as he drove. "Are you okay to drive?"

"Yeah."

"I love those drinks. They're sooo good." She giggled giddily.

"Where to? Your place?"

He hoped to be alone with her and not performing for the press so he could discern what was real and what was an act on her part.

"Oh, Nick." She sighed but said no more.

He felt himself unwinding. A crowd was great when he was on stage controlling it, but being in the midst of it made him feel smothered. He wasn't used to it. The North Pole was just a small town when you thought about it, and that was where he'd grown up. Crowds fed his adrenaline, but he needed downtime to re-energize.

"So." Isabella turned in her seat, and he felt her looking at him. "What are you thinking?"

Seriously? He glanced at her. How could she not know what he was thinking? Girls didn't make any sense sometimes.

"We might get some press. I'm pretty sure they got a good picture of us. That's what I think," Isabella continued. "I hate those picture stalkers, but now we can use them to our advantage. Robin says this will be great publicity for the tour. That's what it's all about."

She stretched.

"Right."

His mind was going around in circles, trying to sort out this game within a game. Was she giving him subtle messages he was supposed to pick up on?

"I feel relaxed but not tired. Sometimes I stay up late and write. I just can't go to sleep early. What do you feel like doing?"

He scowled. Why was she playing these mind games with him? He didn't get what she was doing. She had to recognize that they were the perfect rock couple.

"Oh, Nick." Isabella touched his face again. "You get me in a way that nobody else does. Too bad we can't mix business with pleasure, but you know my rule."

"Right, well, I have rules too. Rock chicks are crazy," he responded irritably.

She let out a melodious laugh, and it further annoyed him.

Nick stopped before the gate to her new house. She pressed the code into the keypad and he drove up to her door.

"Here you go."

"You're not coming in?" she asked, looking hurt. "Are you mad at me for something? We're still friends and I trust you. That's why we can do this together. It's good for both of us." She waited, but he persisted in sulking. "Let's face it, Nick. Our careers and our music are more important to us than any fleeting thing."

Nick glanced at her.

"Let's not complicate a great friendship and collaboration by doing something stupid," Isabella rationalized. "Let's just have fun with this. It'll be good for both of us, and we'll get some free PR. That's what it's about. If we keep our heads, we'll both benefit."

"Right," he said grudgingly.

"Okay then. Good night."

Isabella got out of the car, and Nick watched her sashay up to her front door. She turned and gave him a little wave.

Nick pulled away quickly. He was growing tired of waiting for her to surrender to her true feelings, though he knew it'd be worth it.

14 *Emotional Clutter*

Tina sat at her desk and stared at the business card in her hand. She'd stuck her hand in her purse for lip balm and the sharp corner had jabbed her finger. Jill Graham of *Modern Woman's World* magazine. She'd seemed nice enough. Thankfully, she hadn't contacted Tina since the wedding.

It had taken days, but Tina had finally gotten through all her voicemails and emails and responded to those that required it. She'd caught up on her sleep too. This was the first day that she felt back to normal.

The sleighs had required some maintenance. All the runners had been waxed and some harnesses had been replaced. She'd also had the seat cushions replaced. They'd flattened and molded to her father's body over the years. It had been comforting the first time she'd sat on them, but now she felt more confident in her role.

She was debating whether to go to John and Courtney's wedding. It would be an opportunity to see George, but she dreaded the long flight and didn't feel comfortable leaving again so soon. Walter could certainly handle anything that came up, but this was her job. It wasn't fair of her to rely on him so much. He had his own job to do.

Tina looked at the calendar on her desk. If she didn't go, it'd be months before she'd see George again. The thought of him still made butterflies flutter lightly in her stomach. She smiled at the memory of their honeymoon. It had been a dream come true. Every day had been perfect. She longed to be with him, but it'd be agony to have such a brief reunion and have to part again. And then she'd have to recover from the trip all over again.

"So deep in thought."

Tina looked up into the blue eyes of Kai. He approached from the doorway. She was surprised she hadn't heard him. He wore a gray coat that fell below his knees and a green scarf loosely encircled his neck. His long blond hair framed his face, and he smiled that irresistible smile. And for the first time, she felt immune to his charm. She glanced at her blue ring and thought of George.

"I see it is true," he said, noticing her ring. "Congratulations to you and…"

"George."

"Yes."

He removed his coat and hung it up on the coat rack. Leaving the scarf around his neck, he sat in the chair across from her desk.

"How did you know?" she asked.

"Some elves at the Kringle Café shared your good news." His eyes fixed on her for a moment. "Funny, but I always thought it would be you and me."

"I did too, Kai," she said with fondness.

"It is what our parents wanted." He shrugged. "You were my first love, but it was not meant to be."

"You were mine, too," she confessed. "It seems so long ago that we were in high school."

"Yes, and you were the one who got away. What happened to us, beautiful Tina?"

"You met George, and I met Sonia. I mean…"

He smiled. "I know what you mean."

Kai could still fluster her, and she couldn't help feeling a little wistful for what might have been. Her entire life would be different if he hadn't gone to Geneva after high school. But then she wouldn't have met George. Tina studied the wood grain on her desk.

"How is Sonia?" she asked, raising her head.

"Sonia. Yes, Sonia is here with me. We are splitting our time between Geneva, where her family lives, and here."

"It sounds serious."

"Perhaps." He shrugged. "But you must know I am happy for you. George is a lucky man."

"Thank you, Kai."

"I appreciated your gracious invitation to the Northern Lights Festival last year. It was a marvelous event."

"I'm glad you and Sonia had a good time," Tina replied. "Oh, tell your parents that my parents will visit later in the year. I know they haven't seen each other for a while. I'm sure they'd like to catch up."

"Yes, good." He nodded. "I almost forgot. My mother would like to see you. She has a message for you."

"I've been meaning to see your parents."

"Yes, she would like you to come and see her as soon as you can. She said there is something she must tell you." He stood abruptly and grabbed his coat. "I know you are working. Perhaps we will have dinner sometime when your George visits."

"It's good to see you, Kai. Tell your mother I'll try to come over tomorrow."

Tina rose from her desk and walked around it. She embraced Kai around the waist, resting her head on his shoulder. It felt familiar. She'd always felt safe in his arms.

"Lovely Tina," Kai said into her hair.

He quickly released her, and Tina watched as he strode out of her office. She perched on the edge of her desk. Why had Kai's mother summoned her? Gerta had premonitions and the gift of intuition. It must be important.

***

"The mail just keeps coming," Lisa told Tina when they entered the huge mailroom.

Tina stood with her hands on her hips, scanning the oversized bins on wheels that were lined up and filled to the brim with letters and postcards from children all over the world.

"We had to find some old bins in the warehouse because we ran out," Lisa said.

They heard a whoosh as more mail flowed down a chute into a full bin and spilled onto the floor. They rushed over and began picking up the envelopes. An elf was pushing over another bin.

"We can put them in here. This one is half empty," he offered.

"Or half full." Lisa giggled.

Elves were sitting at their stations busily opening envelopes and entering them into the system.

"We need some elves from other departments over here temporarily. Can you see who's available?" Tina asked.

"Yeah. At least the letters are automatically sorted into Naughty or Nice ones," Lisa said. "The system that Ken designed automatically sends the orders to the Production department. What a timesaver that is."

"And the new system enters these letters into each child's file and saves it?" Tina verified.

"That's right. Ken keeps refining the program. It's so much more efficient now than the first version."

"That's great. I don't understand how my father ever managed without an IT department."

"I know. Right?" Lisa agreed. "We also have the postcards ready to print out for the Naughty kids."

"Good."

Tina thought that was one of her better ideas. The Naughty children needed to know that Santa hadn't forgotten them.

She turned to Lisa and said, "There are no Naughty kids..."

"They just do naughty things sometimes," Lisa finished. "Like we do when we spend too much time at the pub."

"Speaking of that..."

"I hear you. I definitely need some pub therapy later."

"Let's see if we can help out here today," Tina suggested. "We have to get a grip on the mail before we can begin production."

"Right, boss." Lisa rolled one of the bins closer to the workstations while Tina strolled amongst the elves. She felt it was important to let them know she appreciated their hard work and to listen to their ideas about how to improve workflow. She was so grateful for their loyalty and diligence. They worked longer and longer hours as the end of the season approached. It was inevitable every year, but they were all there because they loved their jobs. Including her.

Tina picked up an envelope and pulled out the lined paper. Large, childish scrawls filled the top half of the sheet. A drawing of a smiling Santa filled the bottom of the page.

Dear Santa Claus,
I want a blue truck and unicorn pajamas. I promise to be
good forever.
Gwendolyn

Tina smiled. This is what it was all about. It warmed her heart and reaffirmed her dedication to the Claus cause. She pulled up a stool and she and Lisa worked in the mailroom for hours before she noticed what time it was. She signaled to Lisa that she had to go. Lisa nodded and waved her away.

Tina rode the snowmobile to Kai's parents' house. She wore sunglasses to stave off the blinding brightness of the vast white landscape in the long days before fall. She'd always liked the cozy cottage. Smoke drifted upward from the chimney, and she anticipated the aroma of something delectable baking in the oven. Like many homes here, there was a closed-in foyer that kept the cold and wind out. She knocked on the inside door while she hung up her coat on a hook.

"Tina! Come in. Come in." A short, stout woman opened the door and coaxed. "I am so happy to see you, my dear." Gerta gave her a tight hug. "My! Look at you.

You are a young lady now and a newlywed, I hear.”

“Yes. I just got back from my honeymoon.”

Tina followed Gerta into the kitchen and sat at the thick, solid wood table as she’d done so often in her teens. Gerta fetched a wide ceramic mug from the cabinet.

“I know you like hot chocolate and those little marshmallows.”

“That sounds yummy,” Tina said. “Did Kai tell you that my parents will be back to visit this year?”

“Yes. I am looking forward to seeing them again. Jann went into town, but maybe he will be back before you leave. He would love to see you.”

Gerta stood with her hands clasped, beaming at her. Tina had always been fond of Kai’s parents.

“I hope so.” Tina sat on one of the benches at the long table.

Gerta poured hot chocolate from a pot on the stove into two mugs and placed one in front of Tina. Then, she sat at the table.

“I never saw you and Kai lasting.” She shook her head sadly.

“Really?” Tina asked with surprise.

“Everyone thought you would marry one day, but I knew.” She shook her head again. “Kai had to go out and explore. Our ancestors were explorers. And now you are happy and so is he.”

“Yes.” Tina blew on her hot chocolate and took a tentative sip. “How are you and Jann?”

“Oh, we are getting older.” Her eyes crinkled as she smiled. “I would like to meet your husband when he visits.”

“Okay.” Tina nodded. “Kai said you have a message for me.”

“Yes. I had to send for you. I have had powerful feelings.”

She gently took Tina’s hand, brushing her fingers over the palm.

"Yes. I knew it would not be Kai that you would marry."

Tina remembered Gerta examining her palm before, but she hadn't revealed her insights at the time. Would she have wanted to know?

"Will Kai marry too?" Tina wondered.

Gerta smiled. "Your life took an unexpected turn. Yes? You did not expect to be here managing your family's business."

"Yes, that's true."

"There have been many obstacles on this path, but you are determined and you have overcome them." Gerta's expression was kind.

"Yes, it's been hard," Tina disclosed.

"You have made difficult choices, but this is what you must do. This is the right choice."

Tina nodded. All this she knew, but it eased her qualms to have this reassurance. She waited patiently for Gerta to continue. Her eyes were closed as she clutched Tina's hand.

Then she opened them and said, "Your brother is confused."

Nick? This was about Nick?

"When is he not confused?" she quipped, and they both laughed.

Gerta released her hand and took a sip from her mug.

"Nick is... he is creative. Artists differ from the rest of us. Some of them have great internal conflicts. Their reality is sometimes at odds with their perception. Nick has his struggles, and he fights against himself."

Tina had never looked at it this way. In fact, she'd never much considered her brother's struggles. He'd gone against their parents' wishes, but it hadn't seemed to affect him. Nothing seemed to bother him. He just did what he wanted and seemed oblivious to the consequences. She'd been angry at him many times for his insensitivity. But maybe he internalized things.

Maybe he wasn't even aware of it himself. She met Gerta's knowing eyes.

"Thank you. You're right. I'll try to be more understanding of him." Without warning, Tina's eyes filled with tears. Gerta silently handed her a cloth handkerchief.

"I don't know what's wrong with me," she sniffed.

Tina recalled how Gerta's insights had sometimes tapped into deep emotions within her, though she had never said a word. It might be Gerta's compassionate expression. She seemed to comprehend without judgment.

"You have been holding in too much." Gerta patted her hand. "You have had opposition because you are a woman. Women are born into battle. We do not choose it. The world is run contrary to our nature. Sometimes we have to fight for our place. You have had to fight for yours."

"Yes, that's exactly right."

Tina pondered her father's initial opposition to her succession as Santa and her uncle's challenge to her authority. She remembered finding the journal that revealed the true history of the Claus family and her sense of relief at knowing that this was the original tradition. She knew she had to share this with Gerta. Family secret or not.

"You're so right, Gerta. My father—well, you know my father. I came up here after he had his heart attack. I didn't want to. I was going to college in Florida and I didn't want to disrupt my life. I wanted to stand on my own."

Tina dabbed at her eyes with the handkerchief as her tears continued to spill.

"You had to find your wings." Gerta nodded knowingly.

"Yes, and once I got here, I found I was good at it and I liked it. Yet, I still had to convince my parents and my Uncle Kris that I was the best person for the job."

Gerta listened sympathetically.

"And then I read an old journal that was in the original safe." Tina blew her nose. "I learned about our family history and it revealed that Santa was supposed to be a woman all along. Ironic, huh?"

Gerta smiled, but didn't look surprised.

"Our family has gone through so much to carry on this legacy." Tina blotted her eyes with her sleeve. "But I think I'm the first true Santa."

Gerta beamed at her.

"Wow." Tina sighed heavily. "I guess I've been holding all that in like you said."

Gerta got up and returned to the table with a plate of muffins.

"Do you remember my cinnamon muffins?"

"Oh, yes. I love these muffins."

Tina helped herself to one. It was still warm. That must be the wonderful scent that always lingered in this cozy house. Cinnamon.

"I feel better. I can't stay much longer because I have so much work to do, but I promise I'll come visit again soon." She took a big bite of the muffin.

Gerta took her hand again and gently stroked her palm.

"It was good to release what was bottled up inside. Now I will tell you why I sent for you."

"That wasn't it?" Tina asked.

"No, my dear, but it was essential to clear out that emotional clutter first."

"What is it? What's wrong?"

"Be calm." Gerta stroked her hand, and Tina relaxed with her touch. "There is a woman..." She closed her eyes.

"A woman? Who is she? You mean that journalist?"

Gerta opened her eyes. "She's here."

"Here? At the North Pole? That's not possible," Tina said. "I told her I wasn't going to... I can't... my parents wouldn't..."

"You are in control now," Gerta reminded her. "Weigh your decisions. You answer to no one but yourself."

"I know," Tina said. "But what should I do?"

Gerta released her hand. "She is just doing her job and you are doing yours. Perhaps they are not so much at odds."

"But my parents…" Tina bit her lip. "What do you think I should do?"

"My dear, you do not give yourself time to think. You must listen to yourself. You must decide." Gerta patted her hand. "Kai said he saw a stranger at the Kringle Café. A woman."

"When?"

"A few days ago. Think carefully, and you will know what to do, my dear Tina."

Gerta's manner and calm voice were reassuring. But Tina had already decided what to do and had made it clear to Jill. There would be no interview. It wasn't about her. It was about Christmas, as her mother had said. There was no way that Jill could be here, anyway. It was unfathomable that she'd found her way to the North Pole. Kai must be mistaken.

15 *The Sound of Bells*

"I want to meet her," Lisa insisted. "I want her to read my palm."

"That's not what she does." Tina sipped her Peppermintini at the Snowed Inn & Pub. "She senses things."

"Well, whatever it is, I want her to do it for me."

"You'll need a box of tissues," Tina warned. "Oh, I so needed this drink."

"I know. I miss these Polar Coladas when we're in Florida." Lisa took a sip of her own drink and looked around. "We're lucky we got a booth. It's crowded tonight."

"Everybody's coming back into town for work."

"There's Walter." Lisa waved him over.

Walter slid into the booth next to Lisa and they gave each other a quick kiss. It made Tina miss George all the more.

"I got you a Polar Colada too." Lisa indicated the enticing drink on the table.

"Thanks." He took a long sip.

"Are you growing your beard and mustache out again?" Tina asked.

He rubbed his chin. "It keeps my face warm up here."

"I like it," Tina said.

Lisa ran the back of her hand along the short hair on his cheek. He took her hand and held it.

"It looks like Rudy's going to do karaoke tonight." Lisa nodded toward the small stage.

The reindeer were piled into a couple of booths beside the stage. Rudolph was talking to someone who was adjusting the microphone for him.

"It's going to get louder in here pretty soon," Walter said.

"We could go to the Kringle Café. It might be quieter," Lisa suggested.

"No!" Tina blurted.

"Tina went to see Greta today," Lisa explained to Walter. "She told her that the reporter's in town."

"Gerta," Tina corrected.

"You saw Gerta?" Walter raised his eyebrows.

"Yes, and she told me that Kai saw that journalist at the Kringle Café. It makes me feel a little paranoid."

"Are you sure?" Walter asked. "It's unbelievable that she'd come all this way. How would she even know how to get here?"

"Don't worry. We'll protect you," Lisa promised.

"What else did she say?" Walter asked with interest.

"She talked about Nick," Tina said.

"What about Nick?" Lisa asked.

"Just how I should be more understanding of him."

"Of him?" Lisa cried indignantly. "He should be more understanding of you. You have this enormous responsibility that he dumped on you…"

Tina shook her head. "He didn't dump it on me."

"But he refused to accept his respons…"

"Testing. Testing. One, two, three…" Rudolph leaned into the microphone.

"How do you feel after seeing Gerta?" Walter asked.

"I feel good about things," Tina replied. "More grounded. Calmer. My head's a little clearer."

He nodded. "Good. You'll do the right thing."

"What are you two going on about?" Lisa asked. "You told the reporter no, and now she's stalking you. You need to call the police. Do you have police here?"

"This place is magical." Walter turned to her. "Haven't you noticed?"

"Yeah, but what has that got to do with…"

"There are different rules here," Tina explained. "Or maybe no rules."

She and Walter exchanged looks and laughed.

"I'm confused. Are you *glad* she's here now?" Lisa asked.

"No. But she found this place, and she's here now."

Tina sipped her drink. "And I know it's up to me to decide how to handle this. It's not up to my parents or my uncle or anyone else."

"You're the boss," Lisa acknowledged.

"Exactly!" Tina raised her glass. "To a good season."

They toasted, and Tina felt good about everything as she contemplated her conversation with Gerta. So much had poured out that she hadn't been aware was pent up inside. Releasing it had freed her in a way. Her father had always paid more attention to Nick, and she'd felt slighted. But she'd never considered things from Nick's perspective. Santa had pressured him throughout his entire life to follow in his boots. Yet she was the one who had filled them. Nick's resentment and rejection of his birthright were clearly reflected in his lyrics and aggressive music. He was still dealing with the aftermath of their childhood. But it hadn't been all bad. She'd been lucky enough to grow up in this magical place. She sighed happily.

"What?" Lisa noticed.

"My family is so dysfunctional." Tina suddenly laughed. She could laugh about it now.

"Isn't everybody's?" Lisa frowned.

"My parents divorced when I was young, and I vowed I'd never do that," Walter said solemnly. "But I did it too."

"If you hadn't, we wouldn't be together." Lisa gently kissed him.

"That's true." He smiled at her with affection.

Tina's musings returned to those that relentlessly churned within her. She felt as if a weight had been lifted since her visit with Gerta, but why did she constantly worry? She was more than capable of dealing with anything that arose. She'd proven that many times over. Now she had to learn to believe in herself.

She took a long, satisfying sip of her drink and leaned back into the cushioned seat of the booth. It was becoming clearer to her how to handle the situation with Jill Graham. Tomorrow, she'd make a few phone calls and go from there.

"Hey." Lisa grabbed her arm. She had a mischievous grin on her face and a sparkle in her eye. "Let's do karaoke tonight. Remember when we did 'Girls Just Want to Have Fun' last year?"

Tina smiled at the memory. "We got a bunch of women up there singing with us. What a fun night!"

"You two were good," Walter declared. "You could open for *Black Ice*."

"Except they open for *Rock Goddess*," Lisa pointed out. "I don't think we could open for the opening band." She giggled. "What do you think Nick would say to that? Not to mention your husband."

Husband. Tina grinned at the word as butterflies flitted in her stomach. Life was good.

"Which song do you think Rudolph is going to start with?" Lisa asked.

"He usually does 'Jingle Bells.' He likes all the old standards," Walter said.

"Tradition is good, but so is progress," Tina said, remembering how stubborn her father had been about sticking to the traditional way of doing things.

Tradition was comfortable. It was a place to begin and improve upon. Yet there were some traditions that should never change, and Tina would honor them.

***

Clara peered at her computer screen. She reached for her glasses and put them on.

"Okay. Here we go. I'm looking at flights. When did you want to go to the Pole?"

Santa came out of the kitchen, chewing something. "What?"

She twisted around in her seat to see him. "What are you eating? I told you I was going to make dinner soon."

"Nothing." He wiped his hands on his pants.

"Please don't ruin your appetite, dear." She turned back to the computer. "When do you want to go?"

"Where?"

"When do you want to go visit Tina?" she asked again.

"Let me think." He plopped into his recliner. "It might be nice to attend the Northern Lights Festival."

"That would be a good time, except then we'll be there for months if you also want to be there on delivery night." She swiveled in her chair to look at him. "Tina might appreciate the help. You know how crazy it gets at the end of the season. Either that, or we'll have to fly there twice."

"That flight is too long to fly back and forth."

"Then what do you want to do?"

"I don't know. Let me think about it." Santa picked up the remote and turned on the TV.

"I'll just check on prices." Clara clicked the mouse as her phone vibrated on the desk. "It's Tina."

"Hi, Mom," Tina said cheerfully.

"I was just checking flights to come up there."

"When are you visiting?"

"That's what we're trying to decide. We'd like to come up for the Northern Lights Festival, but we also want to be there for delivery day."

"You probably don't want to stay here that long," Tina said. "I'd have to put you to work."

"We could certainly help if you need it."

"No, Mom. I was just kidding. We have it covered. Things are going smoothly."

"That's good to hear."

"Just visit whenever you want."

"When is George going to be up there? The apartment will get crowded if we all visit at once."

"I'm not sure," Tina answered. "I'm probably going to John and Courtney's wedding. George wants to come up for the festival. He's been to the last two, but he also wants to be here for delivery night. And he wants me to visit him on tour."

"That sounds like a lot of flying around."

"I know. I'm so sick of flying. I was thinking about skipping the wedding, but I really shouldn't. Besides, I want to see George. We knew it'd be crazy like this."

For a fleeting moment, she almost mentioned the journalist, but there was no point in upsetting her mother. And she'd just now decided to go to the wedding.

"Goodness, you're a busy girl," Clara said.

"Yes, but it's all worth it. Just visit whenever you want. There's room for everyone." Tina assured her. "Oh, I wanted to tell you that I went over to see Gerta and she's looking forward to seeing you."

"That's nice. I'm sure she was glad to see you. It's been *too* long since I've been over there." Clara removed her glasses. "Did she tell you anything interesting?"

"Well, yes." Tina hesitated. "She talked about Nick."

"What about Nick?"

"Just that he still struggles with everything and we should be more understanding."

"I don't know about that," Clara said dismissively. "Nick is cavalier about things. Nothing bothers him."

"I'm just telling you what she said, Mom."

"Okay. Well, she's usually right, so I'll think about it." Clara rubbed her eyes. "I'll let you know when we book our flight."

"Sounds good, Mom."

***

Nick rubbed his face with his hands and blinked.

"Are you okay?" George asked.

"It's cool."

Nick picked up his notebook from the coffee table and stared at it while he thought about Isabella. He just couldn't figure her out.

"We're actual brothers now that I married your

sister," George said. "Do you need help with some lyrics? Want me to take a look?"

"Nah."

"Hey, it's just us. Talk to me, Nick," George urged.

Nick stared at his handwriting on the page without focusing on it.

"You and Isabella have been spending a lot of time together. That should make you happy."

"It's just publicity," Nick mumbled.

"It looks like more than that."

"She just wants the publicity." He looked up at George. "That's all it is for her. She's got this stupid rule about not getting involved with musicians. I'm an artist. I'm sensitive, you know?"

"Yeah." George nodded. "I think I can see things more objectively than you, and there's definitely something there."

"Yeah?" Nick raised his eyebrows. "I get that too. She's like subconsciously in love with me but doesn't know it."

"Why don't you just ask her outright? Ask her how she feels."

"She'd never admit it. She's like, in denial. Total denial." Nick shook his head.

"Honesty is the best way to go."

"Nah, it'll scare her off. What I have to do is play it cool, act like I don't care." A plan was forming in his head. "Right. I'll play her game, but I'll beat her at it."

George shook his head. "Games can backfire."

"I know what I'm doing," Nick said with confidence. "What's that sound? It sounds like a bell. I hear it all the time."

"It's your phone." George got up and went into the kitchen.

"Hi, Nick," Tina said when he answered.

"Oh, wow, Tina," he responded.

"I just wanted to call and see how you're doing," she said. "We don't talk as much as we used to."

"It's the distance thing."

"I've been so busy with everything here," she said. "Anyway, how are you?"

"Everything's cool."

"That's good. I think I'm going to go to the wedding. It's such a long flight, but I think I should go."

"Right."

"And then you guys are going on tour?"

"Right."

"How are things with the band?" she asked.

"We're wrapping up another CD."

"That's great. Are you still having problems with Loren?"

Nick stiffened. "Everything's cool."

"How are things going with Isabella? I saw a picture of the two of you in a magazine. You looked pretty cozy."

"That was just publicity. We're just friends."

"Nick," Tina said with frustration. "It's me. We've always been able to talk to each other." She sighed heavily. "Life has gotten crazy since I moved up here, but it took the pressure off you, didn't it? I know Mom and Dad, especially Dad, gave you a hard time about taking over the business, but it all worked out and now everybody's happy. Right?"

"Right. Ecstatic."

"Are you angry at me about something?" Tina demanded. "Is it because George and I got married? Because I hope not. We're really happy, and you should be happy for us."

Nick rubbed his eyes again, trying to still the throbbing in his head.

"I'm happy for you, Tina. Seriously. I just have like a lot going on with the band."

"Like what? Is everything okay?"

"It's cool."

"Is that Tina on the phone?" George came out of the kitchen. "Can I talk to her when you're done?"

Nick held out the phone for him.

"Hi, Tina. It's me," George said.

"Hi, husband." She giggled.

"Hi, wife. I miss you."

"I miss you, too," she responded. "I'm going to the wedding, so I'll see you soon."

"That's great. I can't wait to see you."

"I can't wait either."

"I think I might've found a condo," George informed her. "I'll email you the listing so you can see what it looks like."

"That's awesome. I can't wait to see it."

"Let me know what you think, so I can make an offer," he said. "It's a new townhouse. It's really nice."

"Oh, my gosh. Our own place."

"I know. I should probably make an offer right away. I think they're going fast. I'll email the listing tonight."

"I'll look for it," she said. "Just make an offer if you like it. I trust you."

"Okay. How's everything up there?"

"Great." Tina bit her lip. "Listen, is Nick okay?"

"Yeah. Kind of."

"Is it about the band or Loren?"

"No…"

"Isabella?"

"I think so, but don't worry."

"He just doesn't sound like his usual self on the phone," Tina said. "I know he's right there and we can't really talk about this now. Just watch out for my little brother."

"You got it. I love you, wife," George said.

Those words were music to her ears.

"I love you, too, husband."

16 *Like It or Not*

Tina called the Snowed Inn & Pub and tapped her fingers on the desk while the phone rang.

"Snowed Inn & Pub. May I help you?" a female voice answered.

"Hi, this is Santina. I'm wondering if you can tell me if you have a guest staying there by the name of Jill Graham," she inquired.

"Let me check... Are you talking about that woman from the outside?" she asked. "She looks... well, a little overwhelmed. You know how outsiders are. She's been asking a lot of questions about you. Nobody will tell her where the toy shop is."

"That's good to hear," Tina said. "Do you know if she's in her room? I want to leave her a message."

"I think she went out. I can give her a message when she gets back. What is it?"

"Just have her call me on the office phone over here."

"Oh, wait. Here she comes," she said. "Ms. Graham, I have someone on the phone for you."

Jill picked up the phone. "Hello?"

"Jill, it's Santina," Tina said. "I'm surprised you found your way up here."

"It wasn't easy," Jill replied. "I know what you said in Boston, but I'm still planning on doing the story and I'm here doing research..."

"Can we meet?" Tina cut in.

"Sure. I'd love that," Jill responded.

"Okay. How about if I come over there and we can have lunch at the Kringle Café? In about half an hour?"

"Great. I'm looking forward to it."

Tina hung up the phone and took a deep breath. She hoped she was doing the right thing. She had to take control of this situation instead of hiding. It was better than being paranoid all the time. Gerta said she'd know what to do, and she hoped seeing Jill might help to clarify the elusive answer.

Tina let Walter know she was leaving for lunch. Lisa was still helping in the mailroom, and she'd pitch in when she got back. The flow of mail had slowed, and they were catching up with the backlog. It would increase again right before Christmas, but they were always prepared for that mail surge. All the mail currently being sorted had been stored at the post office for months. She'd have to contact them and make arrangements to have it delivered regularly again when the reindeer were on vacation between seasons. Her father had tried to cut corners by pausing this service, but the mail was now accumulating too quickly.

Tina bundled up and got the snowmobile out of the storage area below the apartment. She squinted in the brightness and affixed her sunglasses before she took off across the snow. She'd always enjoyed gliding over the white landscape, though you had to be careful of drifts and bumps. The air was brisk and exhilarating. It wasn't too far, and it was refreshing to get out of the office.

Tina stuffed her gloves into her coat pockets and hung it up inside the door at the café. She saw Jill sitting in a booth reading the menu. Tina slid in opposite her and she looked up.

"Bean and barley stew," Tina told the server who had followed her to the table.

"I'll have the same," Jill said, closing her menu.

"Anything to drink?" the server asked.

"Just water. No ice." Tina shivered.

"Me too," Jill said.

"They have great rolls here," Tina said as the server walked away.

Jill smiled at her. "So, it's true."

"I have to say, I'm stunned to see you up here."

"I'm surprised to be here too," Jill said. "This place is unbelievable. I didn't realize it actually existed, and I had my doubts, but here we are."

"That's the thing. We don't want people to find it and make it into a tourist attraction," Tina explained. "Think how that would ruin this place."

Jill nodded slowly. "Yes, I understand. But people deserve to know the truth. Don't you agree? We have a new tradition. Santa is now a woman, and I think it's great. People should know that. *Girls* should know that. Why hide that wonderful news?"

"How much did my cousin tell you?"

"He told me enough to pique my interest. Of course, I didn't believe him at first, but something resonated with me."

"Unfortunately, Kris didn't know any better. He had never been anywhere else and didn't understand he was supposed to be discreet."

"I thought it was strange that he spoke to me so freely," Jill said. "Especially after I identified myself as a journalist."

The server brought over two glasses of water and a basket of warm rolls.

"I've been so hungry since I got here," Jill shared, picking up a roll.

"The cold will do that to you."

"I want to assure you that I don't intend to give away this location, and I don't think anybody will find it. This small town is well hidden," Jill said while chewing. "As I said before, I won't reveal your identities. I have no desire to destroy your privacy or disrupt your work here."

"I want to emphasize that this conversation is off the record," Tina asserted. "It's my job to protect this place. I have a great responsibility to the business and the elves and this community."

The server placed steaming bowls of stew before them. "Anything else?"

"No, thanks," Tina answered with a friendly smile.

Jill nodded. "I understand."

"The thing about this is that the children believe.

You don't have to explain it to them or convince them. They just know, but they lose that awareness as they get older." Tina shook her head sadly.

Jill listened attentively.

"Maybe we're not supposed to remember. Maybe this place is supposed to remain pure in our hearts and the cynicism of adulthood would destroy it." Tina stirred her stew. "I just can't allow that to happen." She took a bite.

Jill ate her stew thoughtfully.

"I'm curious why you pursued this story. What's your reason for writing it?" Tina asked.

"Well." Jill finished chewing. "I look for unusual human-interest stories and, let's face it, this would be a scoop. A female Santa? But I also like the feminist angle. You know, girls can do anything. You're a fantastic role model."

"Girls need role models," Tina agreed. "It was an uphill battle for me, just as it is for a lot of women. I had resistance within my own family."

"Who was it? Did your father support you?"

Tina smiled. "You're interviewing me. I'm sure we could have a great conversation about this, but I really can't..."

"Don't you think it'd be inspirational for women to know that one more glass ceiling has been shattered?" Jill pressed. "Girls need women like you to look up to."

"What was your Christmas like when you were a child?"

"Oh." Jill reflected for a moment and a smile lit up her face. "My father used to dress up as Santa. I guess your father didn't have to do that." She gave a little laugh. "Anyway, relatives would come over and we'd open presents. We had eggnog and butter cookies and a big holiday meal."

"Sounds great."

"Yeah, it was most of the time unless the adults started arguing. Funny. I can't remember what they argued about." Jill stirred her stew absentmindedly.

"What do you do now on Christmas?"

"If I'm not working, I'll visit my parents or get together with friends."

"Did you get the toys you wanted when you were little?" Tina wondered.

"I think I did most of the time, but one year I really wanted this doll that was popular and I didn't get it and I cried about it. I wondered why Santa hadn't brought it to me. I was a good kid."

"Children shouldn't get everything they request, or they won't appreciate what they have," Tina said. "We try to answer most wishes, but we randomly exclude items now and then. We have a computer program that does that now."

"Interesting." Jill nodded. "And what about the Naughty kids? Do they get coal?" She laughed.

Tina smiled. "Oh, I don't think there are Naughty kids. They just do naughty things sometimes, just as we all do. I send a postcard to them because there's usually a reason they're..." She stopped herself.

"What? Go on," Jill coaxed.

"I'm sorry. I could talk endlessly about my job. I really love it, but..."

"Tell me anonymously." Jill reached into her bag and extracted a small notebook. She fumbled for a pen. "Let me shadow you and observe. I'll write an uplifting article that will let everyone know Santa is alive and well and we should all believe again."

"It's out of the question," Tina said, and heard herself sound just like her father.

"People need this. There are so many terrible things happening in the world. Let me write something positive and happy and uplifting," Jill urged. "You have my word. I won't reveal your identity or where we are."

Tina shook her head. "I'm sorry you came all this way..."

"I feel compelled to write this," Jill maintained. "I

won't include anything in the article that's proprietary and I'll protect your privacy. I'll sign an agreement of terms for this interview if it makes you feel better. Do you have a Legal department?"

Tina sat there, scooping the last of her stew onto her spoon. Her parents would be horrified she was even sitting here speaking to Jill. Cousin Kris had opened this Pandora's box and spilled out their secret, and now she had to contain it. Jill already knew about her and seemed intent on writing this story, with or without her cooperation. How could she gain control of this breach? What would her father do? No. Gerta had told her she had to rely on her own judgment. And then she knew what she would do.

***

"I'm glad you boys came over for dinner," Clara said. "We don't see you enough. Right, dear?"

"Hmm." Santa was fixated on his plate.

"Where's the meat?" Kris asked, poking at his food with his fork.

"I told you last time they're vegetarians like George," Nick said.

"All the time?" Kris asked. "I don't get it."

"We don't eat meat or dairy," Clara said patiently. "That's how your uncle and I lost weight."

"I don't get it," he repeated.

"Nick." Clara turned to him. "What do you think about going to the Northern Lights Festival this year? George is going and we could make it into a family event. Wouldn't that be nice?"

"Are my parents going to be there?" Kris asked.

"We could invite them," Clara said.

"Then I don't want to go," Kris responded.

"I don't want to go either." Nick ladled gravy over his veggie loaf.

Clara frowned. "Why are you boys so against

family?"

"My brother's going to be there?" Santa raised his head.

"I don't know. Now don't tell me you don't want to go either," Clara warned. "What is it with this family?"

"Most families hate each other," Nick said nonchalantly.

"Nick! That's not true. You don't hate us, do you?" Clara was aghast. "Say something, dear."

"Be nice to your mother," Santa ordered.

"I am," Nick said. "I don't hate you, Mom."

Clara took a deep breath. She'd thought about what Gerta had said about Nick. She'd listened to his CDs, and his lyrics had revealed an aversion to Christmas. How had she not seen this before? And what could she do about it? Why did Tina embrace their family heritage while Nick rejected it?

"You haven't celebrated Christmas with us since you left home," Clara said wistfully.

"This is a Christmas-free zone," Nick replied.

"What's wrong with Christmas?" Santa asked sharply.

"It's a materialistic day that condones greed. The masses are underpaid and overworked and they feel like they have to participate in this competition of excess."

"Yeah," Kris said.

"What's he talking about?" Santa asked Clara. "What masses?"

"People, Dad. Just regular working-class people."

"I will not have you talk about Christmas that way." Santa pounded his fist on the table for emphasis.

"Dear..." Clara put her hand on his arm.

"I know it's *about the children,*" Nick said, rolling his eyes. "But why set them up for disappointment later in life?"

"What disappointment?" Santa demanded.

"You know. Reality." Nick shrugged.

"Where does he get this stuff?" Santa asked Clara.

"He's delusional."

"Nick, please be more sensitive to your father's feelings," she implored.

"I know that Christmas is your thing, Dad," Nick said. "I get that. It's cool."

Clara shook her head. This conversation wasn't going quite the way she'd imagined. She had to change the subject.

"And music is *your* thing, Nick," she said cheerfully. "*Black Ice* has become very successful. Aren't you proud of our son, dear?" She prodded Santa.

"Huh? Fine job."

Clara smiled. "I listened to your first CD the other day, and I found the lyrics... very interesting."

"Totally dope," Kris said.

"Did you call someone a dope?" Santa asked.

"It's an expression, dear," Clara said.

"We're working on another CD," Nick declared.

"That's wonderful. I'm so glad you've found this creative outlet. Remember how musical Nick was when he was a little boy?" Clara nudged Santa.

"Hmm."

Everyone ate for a few minutes in silence.

"Nick, I know we put a lot of pressure on you when you were younger about your future, and I'm sorry we didn't find a solution sooner," Clara broached. "But everything turned out. Right? So, let's not hold grudges."

"Why are you apologizing to him? He should apologize to us for letting down the family," Santa objected.

"Now let's not go there." Clara patted his arm. "We're trying to mend fences. Remember? We talked about this."

"I'm not apologizing for anything," Nick said defiantly.

"Why are you so stubborn?" Santa yelled.

"Stop you two!" Clara cried. "I've had enough of this.

You're going to get along whether you like it or not, and that's that."

"What are you talking about? We get along just fine," Santa said. "We have our differences, like every family."

"It's not a big deal, Mom. Dad's just stubborn. I don't let it get to me." Nick shrugged.

Santa glared at him. "Who are you calling stubborn?"

"Let it go, dear," Clara said.

This family was impossible. Couldn't they have a simple meal together?

"He's like my father," Kris said to Nick. "His face gets all red when he gets mad."

"Boys," Clara cautioned. "That's enough."

"I don't let anything bother me." Kris remarked.

"That's because you can't keep a thought in your head," Santa mumbled.

"I give up," Clara groaned, dunking her roll in the puddle of gravy on her plate.

What was it with the men in this family? Bunch of drama kings.

***

"Nicky," Isabella giggled.

He had his arm around her waist and tickled her ear with his breath.

"Do you think they're buying it?" he whispered.

She put her hand on his cheek and gazed into his eyes for a moment. It made him weak. He wished he could remember what his plan was. He knew he had one, and it was brilliant. But what was it? His mind went blank whenever he was around her.

The server brought their last drinks with the check. Nick was liking this fancy mixed drink that Isabella insisted on ordering for both of them. He was just going to go along with all this until he could remember his plan. He had to admit he was kind of enjoying himself.

Isabella snuggled up to him in the booth and leaned into him to speak into his ear.

"That photographer is still there. Don't look. This has to seem spontaneous. You're doing a great job."

"Right."

Pictures of them had appeared in various entertainment and music magazines, and Isabella was pleased. Their CD sales had increased, and it was generating buzz for their upcoming tour. Her plan was working.

"We might have to take this up a notch," she whispered.

"Right." He wasn't sure what she meant by that. Where was the next notch?

"After the tour, we might have to go on vacation together or let them see you leaving my house in the morning," she brainstormed.

"Or you could leave *my* house," he countered.

"I know," she said suddenly. "We could have a fight. What do you think?"

"What about?"

She furrowed her brow. "The press is going to get bored if we don't give them some drama."

"Are you going to John and Courtney's wedding with me?" he asked.

"That's it," she murmured.

Isabella suddenly shoved him. "I told you I can't go with you," she shouted.

"What?" He tried to recover.

"I said I'm not going. You don't control me," she said loudly.

Nick was feeling genuinely angry at all her manipulations. He liked being with her, but he hated the barrier she put between them. It was frustrating as hell. Why couldn't she simply acknowledge her feelings and drop this pretense? It was clear they belonged together. The press saw it and their fans saw it. Why couldn't she?

"You're whacked," he snapped. "I don't need this."

"You can't tell me what to do," she retorted.

"And you can't tell *me* what to do."

He jabbed a finger at her and took a long sip of his drink. Then he took another. That sure was good. He threw some money on the table and got up.

"Take a taxi home."

Nick chugged the rest of his drink.

"I'm not going to John's wedding with you," Isabella announced loudly. "I'm not going anywhere with *you*."

"That's just fine with me," he snarled.

Nick brushed past some patrons on his way out of the restaurant. He waited as the valet got his car. Adrenaline was racing furiously through him. Crazy girls. He'd never understand them. They made no sense. Hot and cold and you never knew which one to expect. Man, Isabella was exciting.

17 *Champagne Talk*

"George!" Tina threw herself into his arms at the Miami airport.

They clung to each other tightly and kissed, oblivious to the people milling around them.

"I'm so glad I decided to come to the wedding," she said.

"Me too."

"Are you still planning on coming up for the festival?" she asked hopefully.

"Yeah, unless Robin adds more dates to the tour."

"I'm not sure when my parents are coming up yet. I know they were trying to get Nick to go to the festival, but I doubt he will. Things are going to get very busy soon."

"John and Courtney can't even take their honeymoon until after the tour," George said.

"That's terrible. Where are they going?"

"First, they thought about Mexico and now they're considering a trip around Europe."

"At least they'll have plenty of time once the tour's over," Tina said.

"The condo closed two days ago," he said. "I can't wait till you see it."

"I wish I could stay longer so we'd have some time to decorate it."

"We'll have a little time. Nick and I moved some of the stuff from my room at the house over there for now, but we'll pick out everything else together," he promised.

"I can't wait," Tina said eagerly.

"I was looking at the tour schedule and I think the best time for you to join us is probably Boston," he said. "Then you can see my family again."

"That's a great idea."

"Gemma will be going to the concert, too."

"Good. It'll be fun to hang out again. I like her."

"Speaking of my sister, I think she likes Loren."

"Uh oh. Does she know about him? That he's not into serious relationships?" Tina asked. "He flirted with Lisa big time when she was having problems with Walter and he's very friendly with Isabella, probably just to get to Nick."

"I've known Loren a long time, and he's not as bad as you think," George said. "Besides, I don't know if Gemma's into relationships either, and she's a force to be reckoned with. She can take care of herself."

"Okay. I hope you're right," Tina said. "Oh, there's my suitcase."

George pulled her flowered suitcase off the baggage carousel. "Let's get out of here."

Tina followed George outside to the tiered parking garage. She noticed a young woman staring and pointing them out to her friend. George was ahead of her and hadn't seemed to notice. Did they recognize him from the band?

"I've seen a lot of pictures of Nick and Isabella in the magazines," Tina said once they were settled in the car.

"It's for publicity."

"But I thought he really liked her."

"He does. She's playing with him, or he's playing with her. I don't know what their game is."

"I don't understand why people make things so complicated."

"Some people like drama." He shrugged.

"I'm glad we don't have that problem." She dug in her purse. "I'm going to make a list of things we need to buy for our new place."

"Hey, whatever happened with that reporter?" George wondered.

Tina looked up. "What do you think I should do about it?"

"I think it's totally your decision and I'll support whatever you do."

"Yes, but what do you think?" she emphasized. She

was truly interested in his opinion.

"I don't know. I'm not qualified to make that kind of decision," George answered. "It's nice that Santa is this myth that only children believe, but maybe adults need that too. You know?"

She nodded, listening.

"The first time I went up to visit you at the North Pole, I felt like a kid again." He smiled at the memory. "I felt that childlike innocence and wonder that only kids have, and it was a great feeling. We forget all that."

Tina took his hand and squeezed it.

"But you never lost that feeling, because you knew your entire life that it was real," he said. "Maybe that's why you're different. It's one of the things I love about you. You have a purity about you. I don't know how else to describe it. It'd be nice for everyone to feel that way."

"Yes, it would, but my parents instilled in me the need for secrecy. They didn't want the North Pole to be exploited and I don't blame them," she said.

"Yeah. It's too bad that things like that happen."

"Let's work on our list," Tina said, pen poised over paper.

Fatigue had descended upon her by the time they reached the townhouse.

"I should take a nap." She yawned as she got out of the car.

"Not yet." He pulled her suitcase out of the trunk. "There's one thing we need to do first."

"What's that?" She followed him to the front door.

George unlocked it and pushed it open.

"This." He swooped her up in his arms and carried her inside. "I had to carry you over the threshold."

Tina laughed with delight. "You're so old-fashioned sometimes."

Geroge gently set her down and gave her a kiss.

"What do you think?" He retrieved her suitcase and closed the door behind them. "The kitchen, living room, and dining room are on the first floor. There are three bedrooms upstairs with a little open area by the sliding glass door out onto the balcony."

Tina's eyes widened. "This is beautiful, George. It looks nicer than the pictures. Are you sure we can afford it?"

"Nothing but the best for my bride." George grinned. "Besides, haven't you heard? I'm a rock star."

***

Courtney had the huge wedding she'd envisioned. Tina sat at a round table with a white tablecloth between George and Nick at the reception. Her brother was sulking, and she thought of Gerta's words of advice.

"How are you, Nick?" she asked. "We haven't had much time to talk."

"It's cool." He downed the rest of his champagne.

"No, really. How are you?" She shifted in her seat to face him. "You can talk to me. I can tell something is bothering you. What is it?"

"I just have a lot on my mind."

"Like what?" She noticed Loren dancing with a bridesmaid. "Is it Loren?"

"The band is like a full-time job."

"That's right," Kris said.

"Kris, can you get me more champagne?" Tina asked. "Please."

"Okay." He ambled off.

"I'll be right back." George got up and headed toward John, who stood talking with Robin on the other side of the room.

"Nick, it's just you and me. Tell me what's on your mind. I worry about you, you know."

"You sound like Mom. She's bad enough," he griped.

"I just thought that now that I've taken over for Dad, it let you off the hook."

"It's not all about you, Tina," Nick responded.

She shook her head. "We're not talking about me.

We're talking about you, and I want to know what's bothering you."

He scowled and picked up her champagne glass to empty the last few drops.

"It's Isabella, isn't it?" she pressed. "I've seen the pictures of you two in the magazines, but that's all for show, except you really like her, and she's making it difficult for you. Am I right?"

"Girls don't make any sense. They're whacked."

Tina smiled. "Nick, be honest with her. She might surprise you. And if not, at least you know, and you won't waste your time anymore and can move on."

"No way. That's just what she wants me to do. She's waiting for me to play right into her hands."

"Oh, my gosh, Nick. Where do you get this stuff?" Tina shook her head.

Kris returned and set a flute of champagne in front of her. "What'd I miss?"

"Hey, Kris. Where's mine?" Nick demanded.

***

Tina turned on her computer and began checking her email. It wasn't as bad as she thought it'd be. She swiveled her chair and gazed out the back window. The reindeer were socializing by the main barn. She swiveled back and her eyes fell on the framed photo of her and Nick that her father had kept on his desk.

"How was the wedding?" Lisa set a steaming mug down on her desk. "I wasn't sure if you wanted tea or coffee, so I brought you chai tea."

"Perfect, thanks." Tina pulled the mug over and warmed her hands on it. "The wedding was huge, just what Courtney wanted, and her gown was beautiful. I took pictures."

"Good. The leads of all the departments are in the conference room when you're ready."

"Okay."

Tina stood and carried her mug into the large room. Lisa followed with a pad of paper to take the minutes. All the leads were typical-sized elves except for Ken, who was a "bigger" elf as part of their attempt at diversity. He was the head of the new IT department. Everyone chatted amiably and asked about her trip as they sipped coffee or tea or water. There was a platter of freshly baked muffins on the table. Tina realized how hungry she was and chose a muffin that she placed on a napkin in front of her.

"Good morning, everyone. Let's go around the table and you can update me on each of your departments." She tore off a piece of muffin and popped it into her mouth.

There were some minor issues with one of the mail chutes, which was typical, and an oven that wasn't heating properly in the cafeteria. These issues could be resolved easily enough, but Tina was especially interested in what Ken had to say. He'd been instrumental in creating programs that improved efficiency.

"We might need to upgrade our servers," he announced. "I don't want the system to crash."

"No, of course not," Tina agreed. "But that sounds expensive. Go ahead and look into it and let me know what we need to do."

"I also think it'd be a good idea to upgrade our lighting and thermostats to smart units," he said, looking down at a scrap of paper before him on the table. "Then we can control them from anywhere and it will save money in the long run."

"Saving money is good. Let me know how many units and what it will cost," Tina said. "I'll check the budget. Is there anything else before we continue?"

"We can discuss the United North Pole Workers union contract later. We agreed on some changes for this season," Walter said.

"I believe I promised a raise," Tina said with a smile.

The elves gave her a round of applause.

"I wanted to tell you what an outstanding job Walter and Lisa do in your absence," someone said. "They're very responsive, right on top of things."

"That's good to know. It makes me feel less guilty when I'm gone," Tina said.

"We've got your back." Lisa glanced up from her pad.

"It's a team effort," Walter added.

"Thanks. I agree. It takes all of us to make this work," Tina said. "So, I wanted to talk about something. Other than the residents here at the North Pole, we're unknown to the rest of the world. People think Santa is just some long-ago legend. Of course, children know the truth in their hearts." She put her hand on her chest.

"It's all about the children," someone intoned.

"Yes." Tina smiled. "Some of you may have heard that there's a reporter asking questions around town."

There was murmuring.

"It's true. I met with her and sent her on her way."

There was light applause.

"But not before I made a promise to grant her an interview."

"What?" Lisa cried. "Have you lost your mind?"

Tina held up her hand to still the protests. "Believe me, I've thought about this long and hard. This journalist, Jill Graham, works for *Modern Woman's World* magazine," she said. "I know some parents use Santa as a threat to get children to behave. I wish they wouldn't do that, and that's something I can set straight in an interview."

"But you can't do an interview." Lisa looked around the table.

"I know it's not what my parents would do," Tina said. "But times have changed. With all the difficulties of adulthood, why shouldn't grown-ups have that same optimistic belief in their hearts? We can provide that. It's a gift we can give to the world."

"Are we going to be interviewed?" Ken asked.

"It's possible. I want to emphasize that all of us will remain anonymous and this location will stay secret. I won't let this place be overrun with tourists."

"But how do you know that won't happen?" Lisa protested.

"I trust Jill."

"You can't trust a reporter," an elf spoke up. "Years ago, your father talked to someone, and it ended up in the paper. He didn't mean for it to happen, but for a while, we had people coming up here looking for the toy shop."

"Oh, my gosh. What happened?" Lisa asked.

"They never found us, but it was close."

"I never knew that," Tina said, furrowing her brow.

Why hadn't her parents ever told her about it?

"You can't do this," Lisa said. "It's not worth the risk."

"I gave Jill my word, and she gave me hers," Tina said resolutely. "Thank you, everyone." She pushed up from her chair.

Tina returned to her desk with her mug of tea and the remains of her muffin. She took a big bite. Her stomach was obstinately growling. Had she neglected it today? Sometimes she got distracted by work and forgot to eat lunch.

Walter and Lisa entered her office, appearing solemn.

"You're not serious, are you?" Walter asked.

"About the interview? Yes, I am."

He glanced at Lisa. "I've backed every decision you've made, but I can't agree with this. It's just asking for trouble."

"I agree with Walter," Lisa informed her.

"Listen, Jill said she was going to do the article with or without my cooperation. Don't you think it'd be better for me to cooperate with her? That way, I can control the information better, and she'll be more likely to be discreet about our location and who we are," Tina explained.

"I see your point." Walter nodded. "But I don't trust her."

"I don't think I should make an enemy of her." Tina sipped her tea. "I don't feel like I have much of a choice."

"This must've been a tough decision for you," he acknowledged.

"I'm impressed," Lisa declared.

"What for?" Tina asked.

"Because you're not sticking to what your parents would want you to do, and you're going to take a lot of flak for this." Lisa smiled. "But we're with you."

"I hope you know what you're doing," Walter said.

18 *Café Conversation*

"You can't go to Boston," Lisa said, with her hands on her hips.

"But I want to see George," Tina groaned. She was bundled up in a blanket on the couch with a box of tissues beside her.

"I know. But do you want to get him sick too? You could get the whole band sick." She waited for Tina to stop coughing. "I brought you some soup from the cafeteria."

"What kind?" Tina blew her nose.

"It's miso soup. It's supposed to be good for you." Lisa breathed in the aroma wafting from the soup mug. "It smells good."

She retrieved spoons from the kitchen and brought one to Tina, and sat at the other end of the couch with her own mug of soup.

"This is pretty tasty. What's in it?" Tina asked, stirring the broth.

"The menu said carrots and tofu and sea vegetables. The lady in the cafeteria suggested it," Lisa told her. "It's very nutritious."

"I hate being sick. I have too much to do," Tina complained.

"I know," Lisa responded sympathetically. "Walter and I have it covered."

"But I wanted to see George."

"You don't want to get him sick in the middle of their tour," Lisa reasoned.

"I know."

"You get distracted with work and you skip lunch. Your body needs fuel," Lisa lectured.

"You're right." Tina stirred her soup.

"I'm going to make you take a lunch break or bring you something from now on."

"Thanks. You're a good friend."

"And a good assistant." Lisa slurped her soup.

"That too. The best. I know I've said it before, but I don't know what I'd do without you and Walter." Tina grabbed a tissue and blew her nose.

"Want to watch a movie?"

"Maybe later. I hope no one else gets sick."

"Me too. The last thing we need is for me or Walter to get sick or for a bunch of the elves to be out." Lisa shook her head. "Just take today off and sleep or read or watch TV. Just take it easy."

They slurped their soup.

"When is that reporter coming back to interview you?" Lisa asked.

"She's supposed to be here a few days after I was getting back from Boston."

"You should be better by then. Are you still sure you want to do this interview?"

"I guess. What choice do I have?" Tina sighed.

She didn't feel sure of anything right now, except that she needed to blow her nose again.

"Have you told your parents about it yet?"

"About the interview? I can't bring myself to tell them."

"But you can't let them read it in the magazine. You've got to tell them," Lisa said.

"I will." Tina drank down the rest of the broth. "How are you and Walter getting along?"

"Oh." Lisa waved her hand. "It's fine."

"What's wrong?"

"Nothing, really. It's just a big adjustment living with someone, you know?"

"I wish I knew." Tina sneezed.

"I feel like a giant in his house. I keep bumping into things."

"Are you getting along?"

"Walter's great. I love him. He does little things like leave notes all over the place for me to find. It's so sweet of him."

"That sounds wonderful." Tina blew her nose again.

"Yeah. I'm lucky. I just have bruises all over my legs. He keeps trying to move the furniture around but it doesn't help." Lisa shrugged. "What are you going to do?"

"There has to be some way to modify the house or the rooms or something." Tina finished her soup. "That was good."

"Lots of liquids, right?" Lisa took the mugs into the kitchen. "I want you to keep drinking water."

"I will." Tina yawned.

"Okay. Take a nap and I'll go back to work. I'll check in on you in a few hours," Lisa said.

Tina could hardly keep her eyes open as she burrowed down into the throw pillows, pulling the blanket around her.

***

George sat tuning his guitar dejectedly. It was a bummer that Tina was sick and couldn't meet him here in Boston. Their time together was so limited, and it was frustrating to have this happen. He looked over to where Nick and Isabella were giving a joint interview about each of their respective bands and the tour. *Rock Goddess* was still the headliner, but *Black Ice* had grown in popularity. George had to admit that the provocative gossip about their "romance" had certainly helped sell tickets. They were an unlikely pair. She was the dreamy rock goddess, and he was the hard rocker. But it intrigued their fans and had been a brilliant ploy.

Nick had his arm along the back of the couch behind Isabella, and she rested her hand on his knee while she replied to a question. The photographer was snapping photos, and the interviewer held a recorder. She suddenly let out a musical laugh and bumped into Nick flirtatiously.

George wondered if she was for real. It looked like they had amazing chemistry, but was she merely faking it for publicity or were those genuine feelings? He wished he could tell. Nick surely couldn't. Did she know how he felt about her and was she toying with him? George shook his head.

"Hey, I'm sorry Tina couldn't make it." Gemma plopped down next to him. "I was looking forward to seeing my new sister-in-law again. I like her. You've got a good one." She pushed her long dark hair back over her shoulder.

"I know. I miss her."

"Are you going up north to see her soon?"

"Not for a few months."

"At least the tour's going well. Do you like my rocker outfit?" she asked.

She wore a *Black Ice* T-shirt, black jeans, and black boots. Sparkly eyeshadow swept over her eyelids.

"You look rock star cool." He nodded and gave her a weak smile.

"I like the hat you wear onstage." She picked it up and put it on her head and jumped up. "I have to find Loren."

Loren certainly had his fans. He entered the spacious dressing room and grabbed Gemma into an embrace, rocking her back and forth.

John and Milo had taken off to find some food. There was supposed to be a food table set up backstage somewhere. He suspected they wanted to escape the fray.

Kris sat down beside him, eating a sandwich. "Milo told me to bring you some food. What do you want?"

"Do they have anything vegetarian?" George asked.

"Like what?" He frowned. "I think they have tuna."

"Not tuna."

"Egg salad?"

"No, I'm cutting down on dairy. Factory farming is not something I want to sup..."

"I don't think they have egg salad, anyway." Kris chewed. "I don't get it. What do you want? Don't you like to eat?"

"Do they have hummus?"

"What's that?"

"Never mind. I'll get it myself. Just show me where the food table is." George set down his guitar and stood up.

Nick and Isabella had turned toward each other. Isabella leaned into him and the photographer snapped a photo. Loren and Gemma were gone, and so was his hat. George followed Kris out of the dressing room in search of sustenance.

***

"Is it true about your brother and Isabella from *Rock Goddess*?" Jill asked.

"I'm sorry. I can't comment on my brother's band or any of that," Tina said. "Remember, you can't reveal his identity."

They were sitting in a booth at the Kringle Café once again. Tina wasn't quite ready to take Jill to her office yet. One tiny step at a time.

"Just tell me off the record," Jill urged.

"Sorry." Tina shrugged. "I really don't know."

"Okay. Fair enough." Jill got out her pad and a recorder. "Do you mind? I take notes, but the recorder backs me up. I can't remember everything and I want things to be accurate."

"Okay. I guess that's reasonable." Tina was glad they'd drawn up an agreement that was legally binding, although if Jill revealed their identities or location, there'd be no way to undo the damage.

"Let's start with a little background information," Jill said. "What was it like growing up here?"

"Well," Tina contemplated as she absentmindedly stirred her tea. "I never knew anything else, so it seemed normal to me. I had a great childhood, as you can imagine. My brother and I..."

"Younger?"

"Yes. My brother and I ran all over the place, and the elves were so patient with us. When we got older, we helped work on the production line. My father was usually pretty busy, but my mother always had time for us. She was wonderful, *is* wonderful."

"And everyone around here knows who you are, is that correct?" Jill took a sip of coffee.

"Yes, many of the residents work for us."

"What was Santa like as a father?"

Tina weighed her words carefully. She didn't want to say anything negative about her parents, but the truth was that he'd been a workaholic paying little attention to her. Most of his focus had been on Nick, believing that he'd eventually take on the role of Santa.

"My father was extremely busy. He was involved in every phase of the business. I can't tell you how hard he worked. Now that I've stepped into his place, I can appreciate how much this job demands of you." Tina toyed nervously with her croissant.

"But what was he like?" Jill persisted. "The world pictures him as a good-natured, jolly paternal figure. Is this accurate?"

"He sure liked his milk and cookies." Tina laughed lightly and Jill laughed with her.

"Of course. Who doesn't?" Jill commented.

"He loved his job and didn't get to spend as much time with us as he wanted," Tina said diplomatically. "He made a lot of sacrifices."

"Okay. So, your brother was supposed to continue the patriarchal role of Santa, but he pursued a career in music. How did you end up here?"

"My brother, Nicholas Junior, had other ambitions and talents, as you know, but please don't reveal that he's a musician," Tina implored.

"Noted." Jill was writing on her pad.

"Anyway, he wanted to pursue his own dreams, which is perfectly understandable. I had no intention of assuming responsibility for the business, though I'd always been more interested in it than he was. When my father became too ill to work, I stepped in because my brother wasn't available. But it was supposed to be temporary."

"Why didn't your father come back once he recovered?" Jill queried.

"My mother felt it was best for his health to retire. I was already here, so it all worked out," Tina answered.

"Did you have any hesitation about this role because you're a woman?" Jill buttered her croissant.

"Absolutely. My biggest concern was the delivery on Christmas Eve. I didn't know whether I could do it. It takes a special kind of magical gift to perform the delivery, and I wasn't sure if it would work for me," Tina confessed.

"Apparently it did. So, tell me what it's like on Christmas Eve." She took a bite of the croissant.

"It's magic. Pure and simple."

Jill smiled, wiping her mouth with a napkin. "I can't imagine it. How does it work? How can you do all that in one night?"

Tina shrugged. "I'm not sure. It just works somehow."

"Okay. What does it feel like? You must be going very fast."

"It's pretty much a blur. I mean, I can feel the wind rushing by, and I do every delivery, but I don't really know how I get it all done." Tina sipped her tea.

"What about the reindeer? Tell me about them."

"They're amazing," Tina said. "They're originally from all over the world and completely dedicated to supporting me on Christmas Eve. They're really magnificent and powerful. They know the route and keep me on track. I just ride the sleigh."

"And deliver all the presents."

"Yes, that's right."

"Will I be able to see the reindeer?" Jill asked

hopefully.

"I don't know," Tina said slowly. "They're not comfortable with strangers."

"Do you think I could get a few photos?"

"We might be able to…"

"Great." Jill looked at her pad. "Does the toy shop run all year?"

"No. We shut everything down and take a long break after Christmas for a few months. We all need it by then." Tina took a bite of her croissant.

"I bet."

The server came by and refreshed Jill's coffee. "Anything else?"

"Not for me," Tina said.

"Thanks. I'm good," Jill said.

The server greeted the couple who had just entered. It made Tina think of George.

"I'd like to ask about the Naughty or Nice list…"

"I'm glad you brought that up," Tina said to Jill. "One thing I want to mention is that I don't want parents using Santa as a threat. You know, threatening to call Santa if a child isn't behaving."

"Okay." Jill wrote on her pad.

"I had an epiphany after I took over this job," Tina shared. "It occurred to me that nobody's good all the time. Sometimes children act out if they're in a bad situation. Maybe they're being bullied or having a tough time at home. I wanted these children to know that I haven't forgotten them. So, every year, I send a postcard to the kids on the Naughty list. I let them know that I'm thinking about them and that I believe in them. And I ask them to believe in me."

"That's beautiful," Jill said. "And what about the presents these kids ask for?"

"They get their presents."

Jill finished her croissant and wiped her fingers on a napkin.

"That brings up another point," Tina continued.

"Learning to deal with disappointment is a part of growing up. Life won't give us everything we want, so we randomly drop gifts from production. Kids don't always get what they ask for."

"Appreciation and disappointment," Jill said, writing on her pad.

"Sometimes kids ask for video games or movies that aren't appropriate for their age and we don't fill those requests either, of course."

"Of course," Jill repeated and sat back in the booth. "Why do you think children stop believing when they grow up?"

"That's a very good question." Tina had often contemplated this. "I think children view the world with imagination and heart and, as they become older, reality alters this view. As life becomes more difficult and complicated, a certain cynicism can replace the innocent optimism that allows children to believe. That's just my theory."

Jill nodded. "You didn't have that problem because you grew up here."

"That's true. My husband..." Tina stopped. "Oh, please don't mention my husband."

"Why not? Your father has a spouse. Why can't a female Santa have a spouse? I won't print his name."

"I don't know. I feel like I'm revealing too much," Tina fretted.

"Don't worry, Santina. I promise I won't print anything that's too revealing. I gave you my word," Jill reminded her.

Tina bit her lip. Why had she agreed to this interview? She hadn't even told her parents yet. They were going to freak out.

"Let's talk about what this means for girls," Jill suggested. "What does a female Santa represent?"

"Well, I think it's great that the world is changing and there are more opportunities for girls and women than ever before. If a woman can do a certain job, I don't see why she shouldn't," Tina said. "I'm happy if I can be a role model for girls. I believe girls can do anything they set their minds to, just as boys can."

"But you encountered discrimination within your own family."

"It wasn't about discrimination. It was about tradition," Tina emphasized. "My father's brother, Kris Kringle, has a son and he could've been considered for the position, but the truth is that I'm more qualified."

"You're talking about your cousin Kris?"

"Yes, that's right. He's the family member you met first."

"This is Kringle Café. Is this your uncle's café?"

"Yes, it is." Tina looked at the clock on the wall. "Oh. I have to get back to my office."

"Okay. This is a good start. Let's meet again tomorrow if that works." Jill turned off the recorder. "I think I'll wander around town today. This place is so quaint."

"The long days this time of year give you lots of daylight."

"Yes. I keep forgetting what time it is when the sun doesn't set at the usual time." Jill put her pad and pen back in her fabric bag and zipped it up. "I'd like to come to your office to interview you and talk to some of the elves, if that's okay."

"Let me think about it," Tina said. "For now, let's just meet here at the same time tomorrow."

19 *Realignment*

Nick was feeling used and confused. Isabella still maintained her distance, yet was flirting with him outrageously in front of fans and reporters. On the one hand, it felt good to be in close proximity with her when she touched him and snuggled against him, but on the other hand, it was agony to know she'd pull away when no one was around. He made a resolution. If she hadn't come around by the end of the tour, that was it. No more pretend fighting. No more pretend making up. No more pretend cuddling. No more pretend relationship. He'd had enough.

"Hey, man." He sat next to George on yet another couch in yet another dressing room.

"How are you doing with all this?" George asked.

"It's cool," Nick responded without enthusiasm. "We've had full capacity at almost every venue."

"That's great. But I was talking about Isabella."

"It sucks."

"Yeah. I didn't even get to see Tina in Boston and now it'll be months before we can see each other again," George bemoaned.

"That sucks too."

"Yeah. And now my sister likes Loren."

"Wow. What is it about him?" Nick shook his head. "I hope you warned her."

"She won't listen. She says every experience is research for her writing. Remember I told you she writes books?"

"I get that." Nick nodded. "Experience feeds creativity."

"Maybe that's why you're so prolific. You pour everything into your lyrics," George said. "It doesn't come as easily for me."

"You have to suffer for your art," Nick intoned.

"Hey, guys." Loren sauntered over and sat next to George.

"Hey," they responded in unison.

"Hella tour, huh?" Loren shook his head. "It's wild. I'm having to fight off the fans."

"You didn't come in on time for 'Snow Doom,'" Nick pointed out.

Loren shrugged. "I was improvising. We're having fun out there, right?"

"And what's this thing with George's sister?" Nick asked accusingly.

"Nick..." George shook his head.

"Gemma's awesome," Loren responded. "Besides, she's an adult and can make her own decisions."

Kris came over and handed Nick a bottle of water. He tried to squeeze next to Nick on the couch, but there wasn't enough room.

"Aren't you supposed to be helping the roadies break down the equipment?" Nick asked him.

"I'm supervising," he said, sitting in a chair. "I'm the head roadie, right?"

"Then get out there and make sure they're doing it right," Nick ordered.

"I'm taking a break," Kris said. "What are you guys talking about?"

"The set," Nick replied.

"You and Isabella are hot together. The show is totally dope." Kris bobbed his head.

"Nick," Isabella called. She entered the room and stood with her hands on her hips. "There you are. Did you forget we have one more interview before we leave?"

Nick groaned.

"Come on." Isabella walked over and extended her hand. He grasped it and she pulled him up. "Now, be nice. This is an important interview."

"I'm so glad this tour is almost over," George mumbled, watching them walk away.

***

Tina knocked anxiously on the door of the cottage. She had too much on her mind. She was wondering whether to bring Jill to the office and let her interview the elves. Was it too risky?

Her parents had decided to attend the Northern Lights Festival this year. George would also be there, but it might be awkward for all of them to stay at the apartment. Uncle Kris and Aunt Kandi wanted to attend as well, but they'd stay at the Kringle Café. She hoped the obstinate brothers would get along. And she hadn't even informed her parents about the interview yet.

Kai answered the door. "Lovely Tina," he said with surprise. "Please come in."

"I'm sorry I didn't call first." She took her boots off in the enclosed foyer. "I was hoping to see your mother."

"You are always welcome. We are like family."

He gave her a big hug when she stepped into the toasty warm cottage. She followed him into the spacious kitchen. Gerta sat at the big wooden table with her husband, Jann, and Kai's girlfriend, Sonia.

"Oh, I'm so sorry to interrupt," Tina said.

"Little Tina."

Jann got up from the wooden bench. He'd always called her that. He had tousled thick white hair and a white beard and mustache and was short and stout like Gerta. He welcomed her into a warm embrace.

"I was sorry I missed you last time you came to see us." His eyes crinkled with his smile.

"Sit," Gerta invited. "I will get you some hot chocolate and you can share our joyful news."

"News?" Tina sat at the table beside Jann.

Sonia held out her hand with a demure smile. Tina saw the ring and gasped involuntarily.

"Congratulations," she squeaked out, rising to give Kai another hug. Then she went to Sonia, who stood so they could embrace as well. "I'm so happy for you."

Tina seated herself back at the table. Emotions spun within her and she suddenly felt close to tears.

She wasn't sure why, but she valiantly suppressed them. She'd always loved Kai's parents, and a tiny sense of loss tugged at her. Had he felt the same at the news of her marriage?

Tina couldn't help staring at Sonia. She was in a distinct class with her long, blonde, silky hair and flawless pale skin. She was like a vision in a cream-colored outfit. Tina couldn't blame Kai for being smitten. They were a stunning couple.

"It is an Icelandic diamond." Sonia's voice was soft.

"It's a beautiful ring," Tina said.

"I love your pretty blue stone." Her eyes fell on Tina's ring.

"Thank you. I wanted something with a little color," Tina said. "I'm sorry to intrude on your celebration. I shouldn't have barged in like this."

"We are always happy to see you, little Tina," Jann assured her.

Tina sat politely and listened to their wedding plans. They would have the Winter White wedding that she'd dreamed of having with Kai. She felt shaky as she sipped her hot chocolate and spooned the partially melted mini marshmallows into her mouth, letting them dissolve on her tongue. She glanced at the cuckoo clock on the wall.

"Tina, more hot chocolate, yes?" Gerta offered.

"No, thank you. I have to get back..."

"Excuse us." Gerta looked around at everyone.

They silently rose from the table and left the room with their mugs.

"You came to see me?" Gerta asked when they were alone.

"Yes. I should've called..."

Gerta held out her hand, and Tina placed hers in it. She stroked Tina's palm soothingly as she closed her eyes. Tina waited, hoping for clarity. The cuckoo clock suddenly announced the hour and startled her.

"My dear." Gerta opened her eyes. "You worry too

much. You make yourself sick, yes?"

"I couldn't go to Boston to see George because I was sick."

"Be calm. You have more wisdom than you know. The wisdom of your ancestors lives on in you. Be still and listen." She smiled benevolently.

"Did I make the right decision about the interview? Please tell me. I need to know," Tina implored.

"Every decision you make is the right one. Your path will adjust and realign."

"I'm just not sure if I did the right thing," Tina worried.

"My dear." Gerta patted her hand. "Your life is filled with love and happiness."

Tina's face broke into a smile. "Oh, Gerta. I'm so silly. You're right. I don't know why…" She stopped and shook her head at herself. "I have to go. Thank you, and I'm so happy for Kai."

***

"We tried to be discreet at first," Isabella revealed to the female reporter. "But of course, people figured it out."

"Why be discreet?" Nick shrugged.

"Anyone can see your chemistry when you perform together," the reporter said. "Do you intend to continue touring together?"

"No," Nick blurted.

"Why is that?" the reporter inquired.

"*Rock Goddess* fans are stellar, but we need to develop our own following for *Black Ice*."

Isabella continued to smile, but he felt her stiffen.

"George is married now, and so is John." She studied her notes. "Milo and Loren are the only single ones. Do you think this will affect your hard-rock image?"

"Nah. Lots of rock stars are married and still

rocking on."

"*Rock Goddess* seems to have a little more edge after touring with *Black Ice*," the reporter noted. "Do you think the joint tour has influenced your music, Isabella?"

"I think we've affected each other artistically to an extent," Isabella answered. "Nick and I both write and sometimes our styles mesh and sometimes not, but we've definitely influenced each other."

"I follow my own beat," Nick remarked.

Isabella dug her nail into his hand, and he pulled it away, rubbing it with his thumb.

"Nick is unique, but I think I've softened his edges a little."

"Nick's songs reflect a lot of angst and anger at the status quo. Has he changed your political views?" the reporter asked.

"My songs reflect the truth," Nick said. "We're living in a corporatocracy that wants to repress and control the masses. We need a revolution, man."

"Nick is passionate about his message." Isabella laughed lightly. "He means a spiritual revolution. We need to reclaim our souls and our freedom, and we're making strides, but progress happens slowly. I think we have to be more aware of how we treat each other."

"You seem a little at odds with your messages," the reporter noticed.

"It may appear that way." Isabella glanced at Nick. "But we agree. We both care deeply about injustice."

"Okay. Good. I think that about wraps it up. Can we get one more photo?"

"Sure." Isabella stood, and Nick grudgingly pushed himself up from his seat.

The photographer stared at them thoughtfully for a moment.

"How about a kiss for us?" He pointed his camera.

"Right."

Nick turned to Isabella. This was his opportunity to

show her what she'd be missing because he was so ready to walk away. She placed her hand on his cheek and his thoughts melted. He pulled her to him and pressed his lips against hers. This wasn't a pretend kiss, and he let it express his passion for her. What did he have to lose?

"Wow, great," the photographer said. "That will be a good one."

But Nick didn't stop because it felt like Isabella was responding and not in a fake way.

"I think we should leave them alone," the reporter said. "Thank you so much. Good luck with the rest of the tour."

Nick heard them gather their things and leave, and still they continued to kiss. And it wasn't a pretend kiss. Finally.

***

"You went to see Gerta again and didn't take me?" Lisa complained. "And quit hogging the popcorn."

They were sitting on the couch in the apartment. Tina set the bowl between them and arranged the blanket over her legs.

"I didn't tell you what happened while I was there." Tina was still recovering from the news. She hadn't realized that Kai and Sonia had been so serious.

"What happened? Gerta told you that you and George are going to be king and queen of the North Pole?" Lisa rolled her eyes.

"What?" Tina frowned. "Kai was there…"

Lisa turned toward her on the couch. "Kai? What did he say to you?"

"Now, if anybody's going to be king and queen, it would be Kai and Sonia. They look the part," Tina mused.

"Was Sonia there too?"

"Yes, and she showed me her ring." Tina held out

her hand to demonstrate.

"No!" Lisa cried.

"It's an Icelandic diamond."

"Oh, my gosh. I never heard of such a thing."

Lisa grabbed a handful of popcorn and stuffed it in her mouth.

"Walter was okay with us having a girl's night?" Tina asked.

Lisa finished chewing and swallowed. "He said, 'Don't you girls talk enough at the office?'" Lisa mimicked him and giggled.

"I guess he has a point."

"I agree with you, though."

"About what?" Tina wondered.

"King Kai and Queen Sonia. I can totally see it. They look the part. We should probably just buy them some crowns. Where does one acquire a crown?"

Tina sighed. "I can't believe it."

"It all worked out. You have George now, so Kai will leave you alone because he has Sonia," Lisa said, digging into the popcorn bowl. "Anyway, what did Gerta tell you?"

"I've been so freaked out about this interview. I'm not sure if I'm doing the right thing, and I wanted to see if she could confirm it for me."

"Did she?"

"Not really. She told me that every decision is right because your path realigns itself."

"I like that." Lisa nodded. "That makes me feel better about all the insane things I've done."

"Your decisions are no worse than some of mine."

"We suffer from temporary insanity sometimes."

"That's the truth," Tina said.

"I wish the pub wasn't so far away. Don't you feel like a nice Peppermintini?" Lisa asked.

"Always. But I don't feel like bundling up and going all the way over there. We should just watch this chick flick on TV."

"Fine," Lisa said sullenly. "But I really wish I had a Polar Colada right about now."

"Speaking of bad decisions, what do you really think about this interview?" Tina asked her. "Do you think it's a mistake?

Lisa shrugged. "I think you didn't have much of a choice since she was going to do it with or without your input."

"I guess you're right."

"You know what you could do?" Lisa said. "You could totally sabotage this interview. You could give her all this misinformation that would make people not believe anything in the article. You could say things like the elves wear pointy hats and little bells on their shoes. You could feed her all the clichés and tell her they're true."

"The elves used to wear pointy hats and bells on their shoes years ago."

"They did?"

"No!" Tina cried. "See you believed it too." She laughed heartily.

Lisa threw popcorn at her. "I knew it!"

Tina threw popcorn back. "I'm not going to lie to her. I gave her my word."

"I'll lie to her!" Lisa squealed.

"We're not going to lie to her. You're a terrible liar, anyway." Tina giggled, and pulled popcorn out of her hair.

20 *Abominable*

Jill pushed her glasses up on her nose. "This is the big day that I get to see everything. Do you mind if I take a few pictures?"

"Let's play it by ear," Tina said.

"I wish I had hair like yours." Jill touched her own. "Mine is so dull."

"Are you kidding?" Tina responded. "I feel like a black-and-white photo sometimes. That's why I wanted a blue ring."

"It's pretty."

"Thanks." Tina gazed at it for a moment, thinking of George.

"So, this is Santa's office." Jill scanned the room. "It looks like any office."

"What did you expect?"

"I don't know." Jill laughed. "But I can't wait to see everything."

"Okay, let's get the tour started." Tina smiled at her enthusiasm. "Walter's office is right next door. He's the foreman of the United North Pole Workers union, which represents the elves and reindeer. We fully support the UNPW."

"A union." Jill wrote on her notepad as they strolled to his office.

"Walter, this is Jill. Jill, this is Walter. I don't know whether you remember seeing him at the wedding. I can't tell you how indispensable he is. He's been with us a long time and worked with my father."

Walter looked up from his computer and gave a brief wave.

"You worked with her father?"

"Yes. I did."

Lisa approached from the hallway, grasping a coffee mug.

"You met my assistant, Lisa, at the wedding," Tina reminded her.

"We've also spoken on the phone." Lisa extended her hand.

"Yes." Jill shook her hand.

"Nice to meet you," Walter called as they continued down the hall.

"Have a fun tour," Lisa said and disappeared into Walter's office.

"She also assists Walter," Tina explained as they walked. "There's a conference room and an orientation room for training new hires on this floor." They peeked into these empty rooms.

"How often do you hire?"

"We haven't had to hire any new elves for a few years because we've become more efficient."

"How did you achieve that?"

"Our engineer was able to modify and improve the old machinery, and our IT department created programs that helped organize all our data better," Tina said with pride.

She showed Jill the toy shop where elves diligently attended to the production line and the warehouse where workers navigated forklifts to move and stack heavy boxes. They stopped at the IT department and she introduced Jill to Amy and Ken where Jill asked them questions and jotted on her pad.

"Wow, look at all this mail," Jill marveled when they stepped into the mailroom.

"This is where it all begins," Tina said.

"Do you ever read any of these letters?"

"I can't read all of them. There are too many. I wish I could, but I like to come down here whenever I have time and read as many as I can. They remind me of why I'm here," Tina said. "Would you like to read some of them?"

"Can I? That'd be great."

Tina took a handful of mail from a workstation, and they seated themselves at a small desk. She turned on a lamp and they each tore open an envelope, reading silently at first.

"Listen to this one." Jill read it out loud.

Dear Santa,
I'm 7 and all I want is a puppy so much. I promise to feed her every day and walk her. I will play with her so she won't be bored and love her. I want a puppy who can sleep in my bed with me and protect me from monsters at night. Please, please. I have been good most of the time, except I hit my sister once when she bit me. I love you so much.
Haley

Tina smiled.

"That's so cute," Jill said. "Will she get a puppy?"

"We'll look into it. We have to make sure it works for the family," Tina explained. "The Research & Coordination department does that."

Jill nodded and wrote on her pad.

"Here's a tough one." Tina read the paper in her hand out loud.

Dear Santa,
I hope you can give us a Christmas tree this year. My mother said we can't afford one. I wish we could have a big tree with lights and decorations like the ones in commercials. We never had a pretty tree. I'm always good and get good grades. I would like a big dinner with my Grandma there. She lives far away.
Beatrice

"What about that one?" Jill wondered. "What can you do for her?"

"We get lots of letters from kids whose families don't have much money," Tina said. "Research & Coordination will get in touch with a local charity that can give them a tree and a holiday meal, and we'll find out where her grandmother is."

"That's wonderful," Jill said. "Okay. Listen to this one."

Dear Mr. Claus,
I don't like my sister. Can you get rid of her? I would be good if she didn't bug me.
Bobby

Jill and Tina laughed.
"What do you do about that one?" Jill asked.
"I have a feeling Bobby may be on our Naughty list," Tina said with a grin. "We'll look into it. How about this one?"

Dear Santa Claus,
I want a whole set of Matchbox cars so I can race them and a track and tools like my Dad so I can fix them and a sled and cookies and a little brother to play with. I know I have to be good. I try.
Morris

"We can't do much about the little brother." Tina frowned.
Jill smiled. "I think I'd be down here all day reading these if I were you."
"I know. It's hard to stop," Tina admitted.
"Here's one." Jill read it out loud.

Dear Santa,
I want to be a Jedi Master. That's what I was for Halloween, but I want to be a REAL Jedi Master. And I want all the movies. I think I been good, but ask my mother. Not my father.
Casey

Jill began laughing so hard, she had to wipe tears from her eyes. Tina handed her a tissue.
"Now you know why we keep boxes of tissues all

over the mailroom. For the funny ones and the sad ones," Tina said. "One more and then we should go have lunch."

Dear Santa,
I love you so much. Please give a bicycle to my friend Amber so we can ride bikes together. I don't need nothing. Thank you. Maybe you can give me the last Harry Potter book. That's all. I hope you have a nice Christmas. I want to spend more time with my Mom and Dad. Merry Christmas!
Love,
Tricia

"How sweet," Jill commented. "I can see how this job would be so fulfilling."

They returned the letters to the workstation and walked over to the cafeteria, where they ordered lunch from the menu.

"This place is huge," Jill said.

"We have other departments such as Purchasing, Parts & Repair, and Administration where we keep all our records and files, but I wanted to show you the ones that people find the most interesting."

"Do you have many visitors?"

"Not really, but we give new employees a tour," Tina said. "And sometimes the local schools bring the children over for a look at the toy shop."

"I noticed that not all of your employees are elves." Jill took a bite of her sandwich.

"We call all of them elves, but you're right; we hired some bigger elves for diversity. Like Ken."

"And your living quarters are also in this building?"

"That's correct. There's an apartment on the top floor at the other end of the building. That's where I grew up and it's where I live now," she answered.

"What else is on the top floor besides the offices?"

"We have a personal storage area up there and a

large room that we use for employee events.”

“This food is wonderful. You’re really self-sufficient here,” Jill noted with awe.

“We have to be. It’s also important to me that this is a good place to work and the elves are treated well,” Tina stressed.

“I’m impressed that all the employees, or elves, seem to know you. That tells me you’re not only accessible but a hands-on kind of manager.”

“A lot of the elves have been working here for a long time and remember me as a little girl when I used to play in the toy shop,” Tina said. “When I got older, I helped out and worked alongside them. This place has been my entire life. I have wonderful memories here. We’re like a big family.”

“It sounds like an idyllic childhood.”

“In many ways, it was.”

Jill pulled out her camera. “I got a great picture in the mailroom with all the bins filled to the brim with mail and a long shot of the production line. Can I get a shot of the outside of the building?”

Tina shook her head. “That’s not a good idea. I don’t want the people who come here looking for us to recognize it. You may have noticed that there’s no sign outside the building. Only the locals know where we are.”

“Does that happen? Do people try to find you?”

“Not often, but you can’t be too careful.”

“I understand. I made sure not to get a clear shot of anyone’s face in the pictures.” Jill placed her camera back in her bag. “How about the reindeer? I’d like to meet them and get a picture.”

“I don’t think that will be possible,” Tina said slowly. “They’re very… sensitive, and they don’t like strangers. But I’ll tell you what. You can see them from my office window and take a picture from there.”

“Oh.” Jill perked up. “That’d be fantastic.”

Tina smiled. Everyone was always eager to see the

reindeer.

****

"What's up with your sister?" Loren asked George at rehearsal.

"Gemma?" he said with surprise. "Why?"

"I haven't heard from her. She said she'd come down to Florida to visit. Did she say anything to you about it?"

George shook his head. "I won't be here. I'm leaving to visit Tina."

"She hasn't said anything to you?"

"Just text or call her," George advised.

"I did, but she's not answering."

"She might be working on a book. Sometimes she has a deadline."

"That has to be it." Loren nodded. "Yeah, I bet that's it."

George was relieved that his sister had the good sense not to get involved with Loren, but he kept that thought to himself.

"Hey, you really like her," Milo remarked. "Don't tell me I'm going to lose you, too. What about all your devoted groupies? You don't want to neglect them, do you?"

Loren frowned. "This is different."

"Am I going to be the only single one left?" Milo groaned.

"Don't be so dramatic," John chided him. "Only George and I are married."

"And not even to each other," Milo joked.

"Seriously…"

"Seriously, I'm disappointed in you guys," Milo said. "Where's your rebel spirit?"

"Nick is only doing it for publicity for the band," John reminded him. "He's not in a real relationship with Isabella."

"Yeah, it's a real sacrifice. I can see he hates every minute." Milo chuckled.

"I think it actually helped sales," John said. "What do you think, Nick? Has Robin said anything about it?"

"Huh?" Nick looked up from his notebook.

"The publicity with Isabella. Do you think it's helping sales?" John repeated.

They were used to Nick's absentmindedness.

"Right. Robin says it was good PR and boosted sales for both bands," he said distractedly.

He looked down at his doodling. It was a woman with long hair. He scribbled over it.

"As long as it's not real," Milo said. "I can't lose you too, man."

"Marriage is cool," John said.

"I like being married," George agreed.

"How can you tell?" John asked. "You're never together."

"Maybe that's why you get along so well," Milo said sardonically.

"Was your sister seeing anyone in Boston?" Loren asked George. "I don't want to waste my time."

He shrugged. "Not that I know of."

"Don't you guys talk? Does she tell you if she's involved with someone?" Loren questioned.

"Sometimes." George didn't know what else to say. "She's probably busy. I'm sure she'll call or text you soon."

"Maybe I should call her again." Loren muttered, looking at his phone.

George shook his head. Why did everyone play games? He didn't see the point. He couldn't wait to see Tina. It had been too long. He was looking forward to the Northern Lights Festival. His new in-laws would be there too this year. He still couldn't believe that his father-in-law was Santa.

***

"Pub conversation is off the record," Lisa proclaimed. "What's said at the pub, stays at the pub."

"Okay." Jill smiled and sipped her Polar Colada.

"This is a pretty quiet night. The reindeer aren't even here," Tina observed.

"I saw them here one night," Jill remembered. "They were pretty rowdy."

"That's a good word for them." Lisa giggled. "Rowdy reindeer. Say that fast three times after a few drinks."

"This place is unbelievable. I just can't get over it." Jill shook her head.

"The pub?" Lisa asked.

"This whole place. The North Pole."

"Oh, yeah. It blew my mind when I first got here," she shared. "I surprised Tina, but I think I was more surprised than she was."

"Outsiders react that way when they first get here." Tina swished her Peppermintini in the cocktail glass. "It's funny. No one has trouble believing it when they're a kid."

"Well, I want to thank you, Tina, for letting me do this interview and for trusting me." Jill raised her glass in a toast and the three of them clinked glasses. "If my editor likes it, it will run in the December issue."

"Will you let me read it first?" Tina asked.

"I never let my subjects read an article before publication," Jill answered. "But I might be able to make an exception."

"I'd appreciate that."

"I wish I could've interviewed your parents and your husband," Jill said.

Lisa laughed softly, and Tina gave her a furtive look.

"That wouldn't have been a good idea," Tina told her. "My father doesn't trust reporters."

Jill shrugged. "Oh, well. I got plenty for a good article." She pulled her camera out of her oversized bag. "Can I take a picture of you two? It's just for me."

"Umm." Tina thought while she took a sip of her delicious drink.

"How about a picture of the three of us?" Lisa suggested.

"That's a good idea," Tina agreed.

They squished together in the booth, and Jill took a selfie with them. She peered at it and showed it to them.

"It came out great. Thanks." Jill set her phone on the table.

The front door swung open and a freezing draft swirled into the room and chilled them. An enormous white mass with dark eyes glided past them, leaving a watery trail.

"Tina. Ladies," it greeted them.

"Hi, Abominable," Tina responded.

He disappeared behind the frosted door of the cold room. The bartender appeared and mopped up the water and sloughed off globs of white.

"Why doesn't he use the outside entrance into the cold room?" Tina asked him.

"I don't know." He shrugged. "He probably wants to see who's here."

"Oh, my gosh!" Lisa cried out. "That's the first time I've seen Abominable."

"That was really... he's really..." Jill stuttered.

"Yes, he's real," Tina assured her.

"I can't get over this place." Jill took a long sip of her drink. "Nobody will ever believe this." She shook her head.

"You saw it with your own eyes," Lisa said.

Tina was used to these things. She'd grown up with elves, talking reindeer, and animated snow people. Magic was an ordinary event here. The reaction of outsiders amused her. Not that there were many who ventured to the North Pole.

"So, Jill," Lisa said. "Tell us about yourself. It's just us girls."

"Like what?" She stirred her drink with a straw.

"Do you have a boyfriend, husband, or partner? Kids?"

"None of the above."

Lisa leaned back in disappointment. "Come on. Give me something."

"I'm divorced."

"I'm sorry to hear that," Tina said sincerely.

Jill waved her hand. "I'm over it."

"What happened?" Lisa asked. "Did that jerk cheat on you?"

"Lisa," Tina reproached. "I'm sure she doesn't want to talk about it."

"I don't know. It just didn't work out," Jill said. "I hate to be negative, but I'm cynical about relationships."

"I totally get that." Lisa nodded.

"I don't agree," Tina said. "Most relationships work out. You just have to find the right person."

"She's a newlywed," Lisa said to Jill.

"Lisa, you're in a happy relationship with a great guy," Tina said. "Why are you cynical?"

"I don't think of it as being cynical. I think of it as being realistic," Jill said.

"What she said." Lisa pointed at Jill.

Tina shook her head. She didn't understand their point of view. How could you go through life with that kind of attitude? What joy would you have? She gazed at the sparkling blue ring on her finger. She couldn't wait to see George again. He made sense to her.

21 *Opposites*

"Nick," Isabella said into the phone, her soft voice caressing his ear.

Why did the sound of her voice always dissolve his resolve to be in control around her?

"Isabella." Even her name was musical.

"Robin said we were successful," she said with glee. "The publicity increased sales."

"Right."

"It's strange not seeing you now that the tour's over. I miss hanging out," she confessed. "Should we get ourselves back in the press?"

Tempting as it was to see her, he didn't want to play that game anymore. It just didn't feel right.

"Nah."

"You're a man of few words when you're not on stage," she noted. "Why do you intrigue me?"

"Don't know." He wasn't sure what to say.

"I can't quite figure you out."

"Right."

He tried to come up with something clever to say that would impress her, but his mind didn't always work around her.

"I've been contemplating my music since we got back. Our styles are so different, almost opposite, but you bring out my edge."

"Right."

"I like to evoke dreamy, magical imagery, and your music is raw and angry. Tell me why you're so angry, Nick. I want to know."

"Uh..."

Nick wasn't entirely sure himself. His anger seemed righteous to him, justified. Why wasn't everybody angry at the way things were?

"It's your childhood, isn't it?" Isabella persisted. "Everything comes from there. What was your childhood like?"

"My father expected me..." he hesitated. "...to go into the family business."

"That's why you're so rebellious. It wasn't what you wanted to do. I understand," she said sympathetically.

"What about your childhood?"

He had to deflect attention from himself before he slipped and said something revealing.

"Are we having an actual conversation, Nick?" she teased. "I can't complain about mine. My parents are mostly supportive of what I do."

"Right."

"It's funny, but you make me think of Christmas. I know you believe it's a materialistic, made-up holiday, but..."

"I reject it," he said forcefully.

"I know, but you remind me of pine trees and snowflakes and Christmas morning and candy canes..."

"That's whacked." How could that be?

"But it's true. I wonder what it means. I wish I could understand you."

"Why?" he questioned.

"Two reasons. One because you're different from anyone I've ever met, and I believe in synchronicity and harmony and karma and Qi."

"What's Qi?"

"It's your life force, your energy," she explained. "But you're into anarchy and rebellion and rage. I don't believe those things will change the world. I think we have to put out good energy to change the world."

"Rebellion changes the world. Anger changes the world."

She laughed. "This is what I mean. We're so opposite."

"Right."

"But maybe we can learn from each other. Is that why our paths crossed?" she mused. "What do you think?"

"It's not that complicated."

Isabella laughed again. "Let's have dinner together, Nick. What do you think?"

"I'm not doing the publicity thing anymore."

"That's not what I'm talking about." Her voice was flirtatious.

"Huh?" What did she mean?

"You're very frustrating," she groaned. "I said it's not about that."

"I don't get it," he said with confusion. What was she going on about now? He didn't get half the things she said. Girls made no sense.

"You know about my rule," she reminded him. "I don't get involved with other musicians."

"I don't believe in rules."

"I know. That's one thing I like about you."

He waited for her to elaborate.

"Nick..."

"What?" What did she expect him to say? Why did she always muddle his brain?

"Nick..."

"Didn't you say there were two things?" Nick remembered.

"Yes, I said there were two reasons why I wanted to understand you. The first is because we're so different."

"Right."

"Do you know what the second reason is, Nick?"

"No."

"It was that kiss," Isabella whispered. "That kiss at the end of the last interview. I can't stop thinking about it."

***

"I missed you so much," Tina told George.

"I missed you too," he replied.

They cuddled in the back of the snow taxi as it slid over the packed snow. All they could see was a vast white landscape in the muted light of winter, and

George wondered how the driver could tell where they were going.

"How was your flight?" she asked.

"It was long. I tried to sleep on the way to Iceland, but there was too much turbulence. Then we had a long stopover and now I just feel tired."

"I know. It's a long flight," she said.

George stared out the foggy window. He couldn't believe he was at the North Pole. It was surreal. Everything had been surreal since he'd become involved with Tina. She was too good to be true and a real-life myth.

"Here we are." Tina paid the driver. "Thanks, Fritz."

They lugged the suitcases up the steep steps, and Tina unlocked the door. They hung up their coats and pulled off their boots in the entryway. A welcoming fire warmed the room. Tina heated soup and toasted rolls in the oven while George unpacked.

"I always feel famished after that flight," Tina said while they ate at the small dining table.

"How did the interview go? Do you think it went okay?" he asked.

"I feel good about it. The more I hung out with Jill, the more I liked her. Maybe I'm naïve, but I trust her. I'm still a little nervous about it, though. I haven't seen it yet."

"Do your parents know about it?"

"Not yet. I'm going to tell them when they get here." She was dreading it.

"I'm looking forward to the festival." He looked out the window at the Northern Lights. "I can't get over all the colors."

"This is such a pretty time of year."

"Did I tell you that Loren was asking me about Gemma?"

"What about her?"

"I think he really likes her, and she hasn't returned his calls or texts."

"Really?" Tina laughed. "I bet that never happens to him. But I thought she liked him too."

"They were pretty tight in Boston. She could be busy working on a book." He shrugged.

"Oh, I read one of her books," Tina said. "I enjoyed it."

"I'm glad you liked it. I think she's a pretty talented writer."

He slurped the soup, and it slid down his throat and warmed his insides. He let the stress of his flight seep out of his body.

"I thought we'd go out to dinner with Lisa and Walter tomorrow night. I knew you'd be too tired tonight."

"Now that my stomach is getting full, I can hardly keep my eyes open."

"I never felt right sleeping in my parents' room, even though this is my place now, but my bed is comfortable and has a big thick comforter," she said. "Just go to sleep, husband. I'll clean up the kitchen. You'll feel better tomorrow."

"Okay, wife." George kissed her. "You might have to keep me warm until I fall asleep."

"I won't argue with that." She smiled. "I'll be right there."

Tina saw his boots next to hers by the door and his coat hanging beside hers. Signs of George were scattered around the room and gave her a cozy feeling. Their time together would be short, and she appreciated every moment.

***

The Snowed Inn & Pub was busy on this night. The reindeer were causing a ruckus in the booths by the stage. A pitcher of beer had already spilled onto the floor and the server was mopping it up. Elves chattered around them and the place was hopping.

"It's good to see you, George," Walter said, taking a bite of his burger.

"It's good to be here," George replied.

He was happy that veggie burgers were on the menu. He wondered whether Tina had something to do with that.

"This is our home now," Tina said. "And we have the condo in Florida."

"I can't wait to see it." Lisa stirred her ketchup with a French fry.

"We're the opposite of snowbirds." Tina scrunched up her nose. "North in the winter and south in the summer."

"Are we almost finished with decorating for the festival?" Walter asked her.

"All the tables are set up. I think we got most of the decorations and lights up."

"Don't forget the mistletoe." George took Tina's hand. "That was the first time we kissed. Under the mistletoe at the festival."

Tina leaned over and gave him a quick kiss.

"I hope they have those Borealis Blizzards again," Lisa said. "Those drinks are so yummy. I've waited a whole year to have another one."

"I know," Tina agreed. "Things will be a little different this year because my parents will be here, and so will my Uncle Kris and Aunt Kandi. I'm a little nervous about it because they argue sometimes. My father and uncle are both so stubborn. I hope they get along."

"Don't worry about it," Lisa said. "Your father will probably be so mad about the interview that he won't even notice his brother." She stuck a French fry in her mouth.

"You haven't told them yet?" Walter asked with disbelief.

Tina shook her head. "I'm afraid to. They're going to

be very upset with me. You know my father. How can I tell him?"

"There's no easy way," Walter said. "Just get it over with as soon as they get here."

"I'm here for you." George squeezed her hand.

"Thanks." She rested her head on his shoulder.

"Don't worry so much," Lisa advised. "You're the new Santa now. It was your decision. You're the boss."

"That's right." Tina lifted her head.

"I agree with Lisa. You're Santa now and it was up to you," Walter said with a nod.

"It was totally your decision," Lisa reiterated. "Besides, Jill said it wouldn't be published unless her editor likes it, so you don't have to tell them yet. I bet they wouldn't even know about it unless you told them. They don't read that magazine."

"My mother's friend, Myra, subscribes to *Modern Woman's World* magazine." Tina licked the ketchup off her finger. "But you're right. It may not be published, but I should tell them, anyway. I have to be honest."

"Girls should know about you," Lisa said. "This is a good message for girls. Jill was right about that."

Tina smiled. "Girls can do anything."

"Girl power!" Lisa raised her fist. "Now let's have some drinks and get this party started. We have to practice for the festival."

"Testing," Rudolph said into the microphone. "Testing..."

"He's going to start with 'Jingle Bells' as usual." Walter sighed.

"Now I definitely need a drink," Lisa said. "I wish he'd sing something new."

"Rudy, nobody wants to hear your attempt at singing tonight," Blitzen called out.

"I'll take requests," Rudolph offered.

22 *Ebb and Flow*

"You met Gemma," Loren said to Nick. "What did you think of her?"

"George's sister is hot," Kris declared.

Nick shrugged. "I don't know her."

The three of them slumped on the couch at the house, holding beers.

"It's cool that she writes books. She's smart, you know?" Loren said. "But I can't figure her out. She was all over me on tour, but now she won't answer my calls or texts."

"Girls make no sense," Nick stated.

"Yeah," Kris agreed.

"Amen." Loren clinked his beer bottle with the other two.

"That's why I'm single." Kris guzzled the rest of his beer. "Want another?" He got up and headed toward the kitchen.

"Yeah. Bring them out here," Loren called after him.

Nick was lost in thought. Ever since their last conversation, he'd been anticipating his date with Isabella. It was an actual date this time, and he wasn't sure what to expect. She was unpredictable, hot and cold, off and on, charming him and pulling back.

"I wanted to talk to you, Nick." Loren peeled the label off his beer bottle absentmindedly.

"What's up?"

"So, *Black Ice* is your band. You and George started it, and I want you to know I respect that," he said. "I mean, I think it should be democratic, but I appreciate the opportunity to be a part of this. You guys have built up a real following, and it's impressive how far you've come."

Nick nodded. Finally, Loren knew his place. He was a hired guitarist and would have to earn his equal status in the band. With the other guys. Nick was the leader and George was the co-founder but happy to stay in the background.

"I never intended to stir anything up. You've got to know that. It's just that I wanted to take part as a full member of the band. It's kind of intimidating to be the new guy."

Nick tilted his beer bottle up to his mouth, pouring the last bit down his throat.

"But you must've done something right. The tour was outstanding. I hope you're okay with me putting in my two cents."

"Right. Whatever."

"You and Isabella, huh?" Loren nudged him.

"It's publicity."

"It's more than publicity. I can see the way she looks at you. She's got a thing for you."

"Nah."

"Yeah, she does."

"You think?"

"Yeah, man. I like her, but she's too high-maintenance for me." Loren shrugged.

"High maintenance doesn't bother me," Nick said.

"Hey, Kris," Loren called. "Where'd you go? Did you get lost?"

Nick chuckled.

"Had to take a leak." Kris returned, clutching a six-pack.

A phone rang, and they all pulled their phones out of their pockets to check them.

"It's Gemma," Loren said with excitement. He walked into the kitchen. "Who's this?" he said into his phone. "Oh, hey."

"We're not suckers like the rest of them. Here's to being single." Kris clinked his bottle with Nick's.

Nick picked up the remote and turned on the TV. The time on the cable box revealed that in less than 24 hours, he'd be hanging out with Isabella. With no press. At her place. A knot formed in his stomach. He didn't know what she had in mind. It was thrilling in a terrifying way.

There was a car chase in progress in a movie, and he and Kris stared at the TV. Nick's mind was elsewhere.

"Whoa! That's sick!" Kris exclaimed as the car flipped over after weaving in and out of traffic while being pursued by a truck.

Loren returned to the couch after a while.

"What's this?" He indicated the TV.

Nick shrugged.

"You missed a sick car chase," Kris enthused.

Nick looked at Loren. "So?"

"What? Oh, Gemma," Loren said. "She said she had the flu and was trying to finish a book."

"But what did she say?" Nick pressed.

Loren grinned. "She wants to come down for our New Year's Eve gig. George will be back by then and she said she could stay with him for like a week."

"Cool." Nick bobbed his head.

"Yeah. I can't wait to see her again," Loren said.

***

There was a knock on the apartment door. Tina and George looked at each other.

"Who could that be?" he asked.

"I don't know." Tina went to open the door.

Lisa swept in and pulled off her gloves. "Can I stay here tonight?"

"Why?" Tina asked with surprise.

Lisa hung up her coat. "I had a fight with Walter." Tears rolled down her cheeks.

"What happened?" Tina wondered.

"Hi, George. Sorry to barge in." Lisa pulled a tissue from her pocket.

"I'll clean up the kitchen," he offered. "You two can talk."

"But you cooked. I should clean up," Tina protested.

"It's okay. Talk to Lisa." He disappeared into the kitchen.

"What did you fight about?" Tina asked her gently.

"That's the thing. I don't even know." Lisa began pacing. "We were just getting on each other's nerves, and then I banged my shin on the coffee table. It just made me so mad."

"That place is too small for you."

"I know. Right? I keep telling him that, and he rearranges the furniture, but it doesn't help." She dabbed at her eyes with the tissue.

"Uh huh." Tina nodded and waited for her to go on.

Lisa sniffed. "I'm no good at relationships. I told him that from the beginning. It's not my fault." She wiped her eyes. "Well, I gave it my best shot. Right?"

"No. I mean, you can't give up," Tina said.

"I don't like this. Why are relationships so hard?"

"They're not." Tina sat on the couch and furrowed her brow. "A good relationship is worth fighting for. Walter is worth fighting for."

"You don't have these problems," Lisa pointed out. "Why do I?"

"I don't know." Tina sighed. "You guys were doing so well since last year. You were talking about everything and vowed to be totally honest with each other."

"A lot of good it did us," Lisa said sarcastically.

"But you and Walter are happy together," Tina argued.

"We were." Lisa plopped down on the couch next to her.

"I think relationships are like everything. There's an ebb and flow. Sometimes things are great and other times not so much. You know?"

"Maybe." Lisa pouted.

"You just have to hang in there when things are going through a not-so-great phase," Tina advised.

George poked his head into the living room. "I put

the leftovers away and got everything cleaned up. I'm just going to go into the bedroom."

"It's okay," Lisa said. "You can be here. I have no big secrets and Tina probably tells you everything, anyway."

"Sorry to eavesdrop, but I agree with Tina." He sat on her other side on the couch. "Just hang out here tonight and talk to him tomorrow. You probably just need a little space."

"Literally! I literally need more space." Lisa opened her arms wide. "Like here. Can I move back in with you?"

Tina glanced at George.

"You and Walter will make up," Tina said encouragingly. "He's a good guy."

"Ugh! Why are you always so right?" Lisa brought her fist down on the pillow beside her. "Do you have any popcorn?"

***

"You didn't want to use the master bedroom?" Clara asked, hands on her hips.

"No, Mom. That's your room with Dad."

"It's bigger."

"I feel better in my own room in my own bed," Tina said. "Besides, then you'll feel more comfortable when you visit."

"Well, I don't know how often that will be. I forgot how long that flight is and how cold it is here."

Santa brought in the suitcases and set them in the large bedroom.

"Dad, you should've let me and George do that," Tina lectured.

"Don't be ridiculous. I'm fine. Better than ever," he responded.

"You're letting your beard and mustache grow out again," she noticed.

"Just for up here. I'll shave again when we get back to Florida." He rubbed his chin.

"I told you, dear, that stubbly look is in." Clara smiled. "Isn't that right?"

"That's right," George said from the hallway. "You're pretty cool, Mr. Claus."

"Call me Santa." He frowned. "I guess your wife is Santa now. Call me Nicky." He waved his hand. "Oh, I don't know. Call me whatever you want."

"You'll always be Santa, Dad. I'm Santina," Tina said.

"I can't wait to see the toy shop tomorrow and all the improvements you've made," Clara said with enthusiasm.

"I hope you're okay with everything, Dad. I do things a little differently than you do... did," Tina said, wringing her hands.

"It's your company now. You can do whatever you want."

Santa went into the living room and settled on the couch with everyone trailing behind him.

"Do you have the heat on in the other rooms on this floor?" Clara asked. "I want to use the workout room tomorrow."

"We have a workout room?" Tina asked with surprise.

"Yes. I put some equipment in the old storage area. Didn't you notice?"

"I never go in there except to do the laundry," Tina responded.

"Oh, you probably didn't notice because I covered the equipment before we left." Clara waved her hand.

"What kind of equipment is in there?"

"Let's see. I have a treadmill and a rowing machine and some weights and exercise bands. And there's a mat for yoga and a big ball to stretch out my back. It really helps."

"That's great," George said. "Now that we know

about it, we can use that stuff, too."

Santa yawned.

"Do you want to take a nap, dear?" Clara asked.

"No." He put a throw pillow behind his head, propped his feet on the coffee table, and closed his eyes.

***

Tina peeked her head into Walter's office. Lisa sat twirling a lock of hair on her finger and they were both laughing.

"Oh, Tina." Walter saw her. "Did your parents get in okay?"

"Yes, they'll be by later. They're sleeping in."

"Where's George?" Lisa asked.

"He's exercising in our workout room."

"What workout room?"

"That's what I said." Tina smiled.

"I remember when your mother set that up," Walter recalled. "I forgot about it."

"It was a surprise to me," Tina said. "I'd better get to work before my parents get here."

She turned to go to her office and Lisa straggled behind her.

"It looks like you and Walter made up," Tina observed.

"Yeah. He's such a sweetie." Lisa beamed happily. "He's going to see if we can modify the house and said we could move if we have to, but I think you were right that relationships ebb and flow. I don't know why I freak out sometimes."

"I'm glad everything worked out." Tina turned on her computer.

"How did your parents take it?"

"Take what?"

"You didn't tell them about the article?" Lisa gasped. "You have to tell them."

"I will. I just... it didn't seem like the right time. They

were tired from the trip…"

"Just get it over with."

"I know. I know," Tina said with irritation. She rubbed her eyes. "I'm dreading it. I just don't know how they're going to react. They're going to see all the changes I've made here and then, on top of it, I have to tell them about the interview. It's too much. You know what my father is like. He doesn't deal well with things sometimes."

"Yeah." Lisa nodded. "But you've got to tell them."

"I know. I just don't want to ruin their trip." Tina rubbed her face. "I'm going to wait until my father is in a good mood and the time feels right."

"Good luck with that," Lisa said.

***

Nick couldn't stop grinning. He felt like an idiot as he attempted to focus on his notebook and keep his head down so the guys wouldn't notice. What was wrong with him? Isabella had a way of bewitching him. He didn't quite feel in control of this flirtatious dance in which he found himself, but it didn't matter. All that mattered was that it was with Isabella. And she seemed to genuinely like him.

Loren ambled over with his guitar slung over his shoulder. "How'd it go?"

"What?" Nick gave him a blank look.

"You know."

"Right. We talked about the tour. She thinks…"

"You know what I mean," Loren goaded.

"He's talking about your date with Isabella," Kris piped up loudly.

Nick grimaced. So much for being discreet.

"What's this?" John asked. "I thought you were through doing publicity with her."

"Is this the real deal?" Milo asked suspiciously.

"Uh…" Nick wasn't sure how to answer that. He

wasn't sure what was going on between them. But he didn't want it to stop.

John let out a guffaw. "Good for you."

"You've been drooling over her ever since you first saw her," Milo accused.

Drooling? "Nah. She's been after me," Nick corrected.

"Whatever you say." Milo chuckled. "And Loren has the hots for George's sister. Does George know about this, man?"

"She's visiting for New Year's Eve," Kris said.

"Don't tell me you're serious, too." Milo groaned. "Am I the only sane one left?"

"I'm single," Kris reminded him.

"Yeah, but not by choice," Milo retorted.

"I like being single. I got my freedom," Kris said defensively.

"Let's get this rehearsal going," Nick said. "George will get up to speed when he gets back."

But he was finding it hard to concentrate as memories of his brief date with Isabella relentlessly floated before him like a tantalizing dream. Her melodious laugh. Her mischievous smile. The graceful way she moved. Her penetrating eyes. Her enticing lips.

He was hooked on her. And she probably knew it. She teased and challenged him. She taunted and flaunted. It was a dance of daring. She dared him to care, to let her inside his world. She was irresistible and he couldn't get enough of her.

"Snap out of it!" Kris hit his shoulder.

"Right." Nick picked up the notebook he'd dropped. He noticed all the guys staring at him while he adjusted his microphone. "What?"

"Love sucks," Milo muttered.

23 *Family Festival*

"You girls did such a fantastic job decorating this room!" Clara exclaimed with delight.

"It was mostly Lisa," Tina said, surveying the event room and feeling pleased with their efforts.

The lighting was low, with mini lights twinkling along the walls. Round tables were set with red and green checkered tablecloths and poinsettia centerpieces. A fire crackled in the big round fireplace. Mistletoe dangled throughout the room. And the wide windows framed the undulating colors of the Northern Lights.

"We never did anything this fancy for the festival," Clara marveled. "Great job, girls."

"There are too many changes. I hardly recognize this place," Santa grumbled.

"Dad, I'm sorry you couldn't wear the red suit," Tina said. "I had to have it altered so I could wear it on Christmas Eve for the delivery."

"Of course you did." Clara patted her shoulder. "Dear, stop moping. You never wore the suit to the festival."

Tina glanced at George.

Clara leaned toward them. "He'll be fine once he mingles."

"Nick, Clara."

Uncle Kris and Aunt Kandi approached. Uncle Kris looked just like Santa, especially since he still had a bushy white beard and mustache.

"Clara, you look darling in your red dress." Aunt Kandi munched on hors d'oeuvres.

"You remember my husband, George," Tina said. It felt good to say that.

The women hugged, and the men shook hands.

"How's retirement treating you?" Uncle Kris asked his brother.

Tina pulled George's arm. "Let's find Lisa and

Walter. They were going to save us seats at the table."

"First, let's admire the Northern Lights. They're beautiful. I can't get over them." George pulled her elbow toward the view.

Tina greeted people as they made their way over to the long windows. She peered down at the barns and could see that light was pouring out the door of the main barn. The reindeer always had their own party on the same night.

"Wow," George said with awe, gazing out at the sky.

Vivid colors were displayed before their eyes. Shimmering greens and blues slowly danced in the sky. Soon Tina would sail through the clouds in the sleigh.

George pulled her a few feet to their left. "There." He smiled and pointed above them.

Tina looked up at the mistletoe strung above them.

"There you are!" Lisa cried.

"Thanks for getting here early and making sure the buffet table and bar were set up," Tina said.

"No prob. Walter and a guy from the Snowed Inn & Pub helped me get the fireplace going. It was pretty chilly in here until then." She glanced upward. "Oh, okay. Carry on. We're at that table back there." She pointed and disappeared into the throng.

"Where were we?" George bent down to kiss her.

Tina loved kissing her husband. His lips were warm and soft, and she felt so lucky that he was all hers. This was another perfect moment amongst many since they'd met.

They strolled toward the table, holding hands. Tina smiled and said hello to people along the way. She noticed her parents sitting with her aunt and uncle, talking and laughing. This was good. She never thought they'd reconcile after all the years they hadn't spoken. The brothers were both so obstinate.

Most of the elves sat with coworkers from their department and chatted with those at other tables mingling freely. Everyone was cheerful, and she was glad. Because after the festival, they'd have to buckle down for their deadline. The rest of the year would be tough. It always was.

They arrived at their table, and she saw Kai push back his chair and rise to greet them. He'd been raised with impeccable manners, which was one of his traits she admired.

"Kai, it's good to see you." She accepted his hug.

"Thank you for inviting us again." Kai extended his hand to George. "It is good to see you."

"You too." George took his hand.

Tina reached down and embraced Sonia.

"Kai, did your parents come?" she asked. "I invited them because my parents are here this year."

"They said they would be here." He scanned the room. "I do not see them yet."

"I see them there." Sonia waved a delicate hand at a table.

"Good. They're sitting with my parents." Tina seated herself between Lisa and George.

"You need a drink," Lisa declared.

"Uh oh. Do they have those…"

"Yes, they have those lethal Borealis Blizzards again." Lisa grinned mischievously.

"I'm only drinking onc. My parents are here."

"Who can drink more than one?" Lisa giggled.

"We could share one," Tina said to George.

"Let's get some food first," he suggested.

"Leave room for dessert," Lisa recommended. "We have those yummy Powdered Snowball Tortes again. Everyone loved them last year."

"Oh, I'm going to eat too much. How am I going to dance later?" Tina laughed.

"I guess we'll have to slow dance," George said, a smile tugging at his lips.

***

Tina debated whether to tell her mother first, but then she decided to just get it over with. She gave herself a little pep talk and tried to remember the confidence her visit with Gerta had inspired. She was running the North Pole. She was capable of making all the decisions. This job had been entrusted to her, and she was proud of all she'd accomplished. To her great relief, her father had taken her improvements in stride. He'd handled it better than she'd imagined. Perhaps this wouldn't be as bad as she feared, either.

"I think I'll work the line today," Clara decided. "They can always use help."

"I'm going back to the mailroom," Santa said. "I never had much of a chance to read the letters before. I'm enjoying them."

"I love reading the letters," Tina agreed.

"More pancakes, anyone?" George asked. "There's still some batter. I could make a few more."

"I'll take one or two." Santa raised his fork.

"It's wonderful when someone else cooks," Clara said.

"I enjoy it." George shrugged. He went back into the kitchen.

Tina grimaced. She didn't want to ruin everyone's good mood.

"What is it?" Clara asked her.

"It was nice seeing Jann and Gerta again," Santa commented.

"Gerta told me you had something to tell us," Clara recalled. "Now go ahead, Tina. We're listening."

"I should go out and see the reindeer," Santa mused.

"Here you go." George slid two pancakes onto Santa's plate from the frying pan.

"I can't believe how tall Kai has gotten. And his fiancée Sonia is just lovely," Clara said.

"Yes, I have to agree with my brother that Tina has done a fine job," Santa pronounced.

"Thanks, Dad." Tina cleared her throat. "I have to tell you something, and I'm afraid you're not going to like it, but I really didn't have a choice."

George sat down beside her and took her hand, giving it a squeeze.

"Mom, you know that magazine that Myra gets? It's called *Modern Woman's World.*"

"I like that magazine." She nodded.

"Okay. There's a journalist who works for them named Jill Graham…"

"Absolutely not!" Santa suddenly pounded his fist on the table and startled all of them. "No interviews!"

"She found out about me," Tina blurted. "She started calling me. She even called Lisa."

"How could that happen?" Clara wondered.

"She promised she wouldn't reveal who we are or our location." Tina was determined to get this out. "She said she was going to do a story about the first female Santa, whether or not I cooperated."

"She's bluffing," Santa said.

"She showed up at the wedding," Tina disclosed.

Clara's eyes widened and she gasped.

"She said it would be an inspiring message for girls," Tina continued.

"But it's not a children's magazine," Clara pointed out.

"No, but their mothers read it."

Santa scowled. "I forbid you…"

"Dad, I'm running the company now and I make the decisions," Tina said adamantly.

"Don't tell me…" He squinted and shook his head.

"It's done," Tina confessed. "We signed an agreement that will protect us."

"You gave her an interview?" Clara asked incredulously.

"I wanted to warn you," Tina said. "I let her take a few pictures…"

"She was here?" Clara gasped again. "Oh, Tina.

What have you done?”

"I didn’t let her take any pictures of me or the outside of the building or show anyone’s face. She understands the reason for secrecy…”

"What secrecy? There is no more secrecy, thanks to you,” Santa thundered.

"Dear.” Clara patted his arm. "Don’t get yourself worked up.”

"I didn’t tell her about the condo in Florida or about Nick and his band,” Tina assured them.

"When is this article coming out?” Clara asked.

"It will be in the December issue that comes out in November,” Tina answered. "That’s if her editor approves the story. I haven’t heard whether that’s happened yet.”

"There’s still a chance we can stop it.” Clara looked at Santa.

"Mom, I signed an agreement,” Tina reminded her. "I made a decision, and I’m sticking to it.”

"Tina, I don’t think you thought this through,” Clara said, dabbing her mouth with a napkin. "There’s a reason we do things this way.”

"It’s the way it’s been done since the beginning,” Santa grumbled. "It’s tradition.”

"But everyone here knows who we are,” Tina argued.

"Yes, well, that’s because we live here,” Clara answered. "No one outside the North Pole is supposed to know.”

"But why not?” Tina asked. "To guard our privacy?” Clara looked at Santa.

"This is for the children and they know it in here.” Santa tapped his fist over his heart. "That’s all that matters. You can’t make people believe.”

"I think people *need* to believe,” Tina said fervently. "People need to know there’s something wonderful and magical in the world.”

"I agree with Tina,” George spoke up. "I didn’t know

about all this until I met her. There are so many terrible things happening every day, and it's made me see that there's some good in the world. There's something pure and even magical. We need these things to balance out the bad stuff. We need to hold on to some part of our childhoods. I feel like a kid when I'm here, in a good way."

Tina smiled her appreciation at George before she turned back to her parents.

"First, you don't need to worry. This is a woman's magazine and it won't be picked up by the major news outlets."

"This is true," Clara conceded.

"Second, it may not even be published, and if it is, people probably won't believe it."

"Nobody will believe it," Santa agreed.

"But if the main press picks up the story and people believe it, then it will be a good message for girls," Tina concluded.

"And boys and adults," George added.

Clara looked at Santa again.

"I'll email Jill and see what the status of the article is," Tina said.

"I'm going to the mailroom." Santa finished his pancakes.

"What can I do to help?" George asked.

"You can work the production line with me," Clara answered. "They could always use the help."

"That sounds great," he said eagerly.

"Tina and Nick used to work the line with us every season." Clara frowned. "Goodness, did we violate child labor laws, I wonder?"

***

Tina sat down at her desk and turned on her computer. She felt a little shaky, but she was proud of herself. She'd stood up to her father. She had confidence in her decision and she'd stood her ground. And George had backed her up. She took a deep breath to calm herself and opened her email. Nothing from Jill yet. This concerned her.

Hi Jill,
I was just wondering about the status of the article. I haven't heard from you yet. Has your editor had a chance to read it? I informed my parents, and they're feeling anxious about it. I'd really appreciate it if you could send me the article in advance. I enjoyed meeting you. Hope all is well.
Thank you,
Santina

She hit "send" and sat back in her chair. She swiveled back and forth, going over the conversation with her parents. Were they right? She still entertained some qualms, though she'd attempted to exude self-assurance. Managers couldn't allow themselves to be plagued with doubts. It was important to be decisive and act accordingly. The elves had faith in her.

What choice had she had, anyway? Jill had vowed to do the article with or without her. Wasn't it better to set the record straight? Oh well, she couldn't do anything about it now.

She read an email about an assignment. She was still taking the occasional online business class. She thought it was important to keep up with the latest innovations in technology, production, and inventory management. She also subscribed to several online trade magazines. She did so much reading on her computer that sometimes her eyes were red by the end of the day. But she loved her job.

Tina swiveled around in her chair to look out the window behind her. The reindeer were outside kicking around a big red ball. It brought back memories of playing with Dancer and Prancer. They'd kicked a ball back and forth while she'd chased it, laughing and falling in the snow. Finally, her mother had retrieved her and brought her inside to warm up. Now that she thought about it, she hadn't been alone. Kai had been playing with her. Her mother had given them dinner with Nick, and then Jann had picked him up.

She'd known Kai ever since she could remember. He'd often played in the toy shop with her and Nick, and she'd spent many days at his house drinking hot chocolate with mini marshmallows. All the girls had liked Kai in high school, but she was the one who had captivated his attention. They'd shared their first kiss, and she'd believed it would last forever. But they'd outgrown each other. And now they'd each found the right person. Kai would always be a good friend and a fond memory.

Tina swiveled back to her computer and noticed a new email in her inbox from Jill. She quickly opened it, hoping for some good news, whatever that was.

Hi Santina,
So good to hear from you. I can't tell you how much meeting you has meant to me. It changed my outlook on life. Sorry to gush, but it's true. My editor was intrigued by the article and wants to run it, but I doubt she believes it. I guess that will be the response from most readers. I appreciate your trust in me, and I assure you that you'll be happy with the article. My editor has suggested some changes, so I'm still working on it. I'll send you a copy of the magazine, though you'll be able to read the article online. My editor doesn't want me to provide you with an advance copy due to potentially influencing the final version, but I'll see what I can do. I enjoyed hanging out at the inn with you and Lisa. Please tell her hello.
Sincerely,
Jill

Tina sighed. It was just going to be a waiting game.

Hopefully, by the time the article came out, her parents would have adjusted to the idea and their anger would've abated. Besides, Jill and her father were most likely right that most people wouldn't believe it, anyway. Readers would consider the possibility that the Claus family and the North Pole were real outlandish, despite espousing the myth to their children.

And what if some people did believe it? What would that entail? Would more reporters pursue them? Would the tranquility of the North Pole be disrupted? Had she opened a Pandora's box of consequences?

Tina rubbed her face. Whatever the outcome, she hoped she hadn't sabotaged the North Pole and the sanctity of Santa. She'd never forgive herself.

24 *Secret Santa*

Nick wasn't sure how it happened, but he and Loren seemed to be friends now. Maybe it was because they were both going through romantic drama. Whatever the reason, it was good for the band. They'd played a few local gigs without George, and Loren had picked up the slack. That was good, because Nick felt certain that George would be absent more often. He might even quit the band eventually to be up north full time with Tina. He hoped not, but it wouldn't be a surprise.

Loren handed him a beer and sat in the easy chair opposite the couch.

"Yeah, so Gemma and I have been talking on the phone almost every night. We have these long, intense conversations."

"Right."

"She's amazing and smart and funny. I've just never met anyone like her." He shook his head.

"Right."

"How are things going with Isabella?"

"We've been hanging out."

"That one is a tease, am I right? She's a master at it." He grinned. "She's going to drive you crazy."

"It's a game," Nick said. "They play games."

"Yeah, but it hurts so good, right?" Loren laughed and took a swig of beer. "Where's your shadow Kris?"

Nick shrugged. "Around here somewhere."

Loren looked under the coffee table and lifted a throw pillow. "Not here."

"Gemma's coming to our gig on New Year's Eve?" Nick asked.

"Yeah, I wish it was sooner," Loren groaned. "When is George coming back?"

"Not until after Christmas."

"That doesn't give us much time to rehearse with him."

"Right."

"Does *Rock Goddess* have a gig, or is Isabella coming to ours?" Loren wondered.

"Lilliana is going to be visiting her family over the holidays, so they don't have a gig lined up," Nick answered. "They rarely do gigs on New Year's Eve."

"You guys should sing together. The fans love it." Loren peeled the label off his bottle.

"Do you ever write songs?"

"Me? No. I don't have the patience to sit down and do it. Just give me a guitar and let me go. That's my creative outlet."

Nick nodded. That was good. They always had too many songs to squeeze onto each CD as it was. The other guys wrote songs here and there, though not as many as Nick. His feelings for Isabella had inspired more lyrics than he could keep up with. She was his muse. He was sure of it. It was their destiny to be together, and she was incrementally surrendering to him. Finally, she was coming to her senses. He just had to be patient. Not one of his virtues.

"There you guys are." Kris came in the front door.

Loren glanced at Nick with amusement. "Where else would we be?"

"At rehearsal."

"Rehearsal? Did we have a rehearsal?" Loren raised his eyebrows.

"I was the only one who showed up," Kris griped. "But Milo wasn't even home. Is the rehearsal somewhere else tonight?"

"There is no rehearsal tonight." Nick shook his head.

"Are you sure?" Kris looked puzzled. "I got a text." He pulled out his phone and squinted at it.

"You got a text saying the rehearsal was canceled," Nick informed him. "Milo had a family thing."

"You don't even need to go to rehearsals," Loren told Kris.

"Yeah, I do. I'm Nick's assistant. I'm indesposable."

"Indispensable?" Loren asked.

"That's what I said." Kris narrowed his eyes. "I don't play an instrument, but I'm indesposable behind the scenes. You couldn't be in front of the scenes without me."

"Okay, Kris." Loren took a sip of beer.

***

Things had been going smoothly. It was nice to have so much help. Tina was glad that George had been working alongside her parents so they could get to know each other better. He had planned to return to Florida after the festival and come back for Christmas Eve, but had decided to stay. *Black Ice* didn't need him for the few local gigs they had scheduled, he told her. She hoped Nick was okay with that. She didn't want to create a conflict with her brother, but George had assured her it was fine.

"Do you think Jill will mention me in the article?" Lisa asked.

"I don't know."

"I can't wait to read it." Lisa was sitting at the table in Tina's office, which served as her desk.

"My parents were impressed with your decorating skills for the festival. You did an amazing job."

"Yeah, your mother told me. I can't believe so much time has gone by already. Time flies when you're having fun, huh?"

"I'm surprised my father is okay with all the changes I made," Tina said. "I keep waiting for the other shoe to drop."

"Oh, it will once the article comes out," Lisa said.

"I'm trying not to dwell on that."

"Sorry," Lisa said. "It must be nice having George around for so long, though."

"Yes, it's a little awkward with my parents in the next room, but I'm glad they're spending time together."

"How long will your parents be here?"

"They want to be here for Christmas Eve."

"Do you think your father misses it?" Lisa asked. "Maybe he'll want to come back and run the business again."

"No, he can't do that." Tina grimaced. "I don't know why that never occurred to me before. I'm sure he misses it and he's bored with retirement sometimes."

"Don't worry." Lisa waved her hand. "Your mother would let him."

"You're probably right. He'd get too stressed again." Tina tried to focus on her computer.

"You've been so busy with your parents and George that we hardly get to talk anymore," Lisa said. "Especially with how busy things are now."

"I know. How are you and Walter doing?"

"Oh." Lisa smiled. "He actually slipped once and said something about when we're married someday."

"Oh, my gosh. What did you say?"

"I told him he'd better not mention that ever again or I'll run for the hills." Lisa giggled. "But then he said there are no hills here."

"Walter's great." Tina smiled.

"Yeah, he is."

Clara poked her head into the office. "Do you girls want to take a break and go to lunch?"

"Sure, Mrs. Claus," Lisa said.

"Where's George?" Tina asked.

"He's helping your father in the warehouse."

"Mom," Tina broached. "Do you think Dad misses it? Do you think he'll want to come back?"

Clara stood with her hands on her hips in the doorway. "Well... yes, I think he misses it. Remember, he spent almost his entire adult life dedicated to this job."

"He seems to miss it."

"I'm sure he does, but it's kind of like when you're a grandparent." She held up her hand. "No pressure, of course. But you don't have to do it full time anymore. You can do it whenever you want, but all the responsibility is on someone else."

"Best of both worlds." Lisa nodded.

"Yes, exactly," Clara said. "We might just come for the festival every year and help for a few months." She shrugged. "If we're not busy. Of course, we'd come if you needed us."

"I sure don't mind the help," Tina said.

"Let's go eat. I love the hummus wrap they have in the cafeteria." Lisa shut down her computer.

"Hummus wrap? I haven't tried that yet," Clara said with interest. "Is it organic?"

Lisa wrinkled her brow. "I don't know. But the tortilla is whole wheat."

"Whole wheat? Really?" Clara's face lit up.

***

"I'm going to talk to the cafeteria about the Thanksgiving menu," Lisa said. "It's only a few weeks away and I want to make sure we have plenty of veggie stuff for your parents and George."

"That's a good idea. Thanks." Tina yawned and turned on her computer. "I couldn't sleep last night. My father stayed up late watching TV and I could hear it in our bedroom. It kept me awake."

"I'll bring you back some tea."

"Better make it coffee."

"Right, boss." Lisa saluted her. "I'll go see if Walter wants anything."

Tina yawned again and opened up her email. She immediately noticed one from Jill.

Hi Santina,
I hope all is well. The December issue of the magazine is out and I've put one in the mail for you. I'm sorry I couldn't provide an advance copy of the article, but I

think you'll be pleased with it. Things get crazy around here when we're putting together the holiday issue. I imagine you're busy as well. I've provided the link to the article in the online magazine at the bottom of this email. Feel free to give me feedback. Say hello to Lisa. I sure do miss those Polar Coladas.
Sincerely,
Jill

Tina stared at the link. All she could think about was her parents' reaction. Jill had promised that she wouldn't reveal their identities or location, so it should be okay. Still, she couldn't help feeling nervous. The article was out there and people could be reading it this very minute. What would the response be? She realized she was trembling as she clicked the link.

The first thing she saw was a full-page blurred photo of a Christmas tree. The words "Secret Santa By Jill Graham" were superimposed over it. She saw that there were more photos interspersed throughout the article and recognized Jill's pictures of the reindeer, the production line, and the warehouse. And then Tina quickly read it, her excitement tinged with dread.

Secret Santa
By Jill Graham

Shhh! I've discovered a well-kept secret that I'm going to share it with you. I know you won't believe it, but I assure you I have seen it with my very own eyes. Our children take for granted the existence of Santa Claus, and we encourage this belief as our parents did for us and their parents did for them. We even use this belief to inspire good behavior. Nobody wants to be on Santa's Naughty list, now do they?

Children write a plethora of letters to Santa filled with their Christmas wishes and innermost dreams and send them off to the North Pole where most of us assume they wind up in some obscure post office in unread piles. Movies, books, and TV shows perpetuate the myth of elves assembling toys in a workshop and flying reindeer hauling a laden sleigh through the night sky. We even leave cookies and milk out for Santa on Christmas Eve. We enjoy seeing the wide-eyed wonder of children on Christmas morning because we know they will grow up far too soon and lose this sense of innocence and pure joy.

But what if I told you that Santa Claus is real? And the North Pole is a small town in which many of the residents are employed by Santa? And there really are flying reindeer and elves and a toy shop? Every child believes these things without question. But you wouldn't believe me, would you? I didn't believe it either.

So, let me relate what transpired. I happened to have a casual conversation with someone who told me something stupendous, something that sounded inconceivable. But many true stories are stranger than fiction and I was intrigued, so I dove down each rabbit hole that appeared. I didn't expect to find anything but a dead end. Incredibly, that's not what happened.

I discovered that Santa Claus is real, though I never personally met him. Bear with me. It gets better. Santa retired a few years ago, and, as is the custom, the role was passed on to his progeny, who happens to be a daughter. For the first time in history, Santa is a woman. She is an efficient, professional young woman named Santina Claus. And I had the good fortune to meet her.

How did I know this wasn't a hoax? Because I had to track her down and persuade her to give me an exclusive interview. I also traveled a great distance to the North Pole and saw the entire enterprise with my own eyes, including the toy shop. Santina granted me a reluctant, yet gracious, interview after I signed an agreement ensuring specified restrictions to protect their privacy.

The organization is enormous, with many departments that Santina skillfully manages and coordinates. She grew up here and played in the toy shop as a child. Later, she learned the business by assisting wherever she was needed. She's a compassionate employer and considers the employees more like family than workers. Many of the elves are second, third, and fourth generation employees and they speak highly of Santina.

This business isn't about profits, the bottom line, or cutting corners. It's about the children and tradition and quality. Everyone takes great pride in their work and knows exactly why they're there. I spoke with many of the elves and toured several departments. Of course, one of the most exciting is the production line where elves diligently assemble and lovingly embellish toys. I viewed the enormous warehouse where these toys are carefully stored for each child, and I witnessed the endless stacks of mail in the mailroom where each letter is read and assessed. Although there is a Naughty or Nice list, Santina maintains that there are no naughty children and that children are inherently good. I found this refreshing. No one amongst us is always good.

I asked Santina what it was like growing up there. She smiled and said she's never known anything else. Santa was devoted to his job, and she played with the elves. She watched her father ride the sleigh every Christmas Eve with wonder. She confessed that she wasn't sure she'd be able to accomplish the delivery when she'd assumed the role. I asked her how she achieves this monumental mission. Magic, she said simply. Indeed, there is magic in the air. Talking snowmen included.

Santina also shared her family history. Originally, the first Santa was supposed to be a woman. It makes sense since women nurtured and raised the children. A magical Gift was bestowed upon this first family so that future generations could continue the tradition. However, tragedy intervened and the first female Santa perished before she could fulfill this coveted role. Her husband stepped in and history was sealed. Now we have finally come full circle to honor the original custom.

In a world where the news bombards us with horrors around the world and cynicism descends upon us, this oasis of innocence and joy is welcome. Why do we stop believing when we grow up? Reality seems to overwhelm us with obligations and responsibilities and the serious business of adulthood, but now we can hold on to a little of the magic of childhood, the wonder of snow wafting down from the sky or a vibrant sunset or sand between our toes. And a benevolent Santina who embraces her job to bring happiness to all children. We can believe again.

What does it mean to have a female Santa? Another glass ceiling has shattered, and there's a new role model to look up to and admire. This proves that girls can do just about anything. It's an important lesson for girls and boys and the parents who raise them. Yes, Virginia, there is a Santina Claus. ~JG

Tina wiped a tear from her eye. Jill had kept her word, and the article was vague enough to conceal who and where they were. Yet it had captured the essence of this magical place and the selfless dedication of the elves. How would the world respond? And more importantly, how would her parents react?

25 *Larger Than Life*

"Hmm." Clara took off her reading glasses and handed the article back to Tina, who had been pacing.

"I thought it'd be easier to read if I printed it out," Tina said. She passed it to George. "What did you think, Mom?"

Clara cleared her throat. "I think it's fine. I wish it hadn't been published in the first place, but it's not bad."

"But what will Dad think?" Tina fretted.

Clara crossed her arms as she sat on the couch. "He won't be happy no matter what it says, but he'll get over it."

"He won't be too mad?" Tina stood, wringing her hands.

"Don't worry. It's a nice article and maybe it will do some good," Clara said. "We'll see if it gets picked up by the news. That's the real test. If not, then it's no big deal."

"Yes, you could be right," Tina acknowledged. "I forwarded the link to Nick and Walter and Lisa. I asked her to find Dad and send him up here so he can read it."

Clara watched Tina pace. "Don't get yourself all worked up over this. This job is stressful enough. I don't want you to have health issues like your father."

"What happened years ago when Dad gave an interview?" Tina questioned.

"Now that was a real fiasco," Clara told her. "Some local reporter in Florida found us, and your father gave him a brief interview. Then he did an article that made your father look like some kind of delusional crazy person who believed he was Santa." She shook her head. "It took your father a long time to get over that one. I wouldn't bring it up if I were you."

"No wonder he doesn't trust reporters," Tina said.

Santa burst into the apartment. "Where is it? Is this

it?" He snatched the pages from George's hands.

"I liked it," George said calmly. "I thought it was good."

"Nobody asked you," Santa grumbled.

"Don't be rude, dear." Clara reproached him. "George, ignore him."

"Turn on the news," Santa demanded. "Let's see if it made the news."

"The news isn't on yet and I doubt CNN would carry it," Clara said.

They waited while Santa read. Tina rocked on her heels with her arms folded, ready to defend herself.

"It's not too bad," Santa said, tossing the pages onto the coffee table.

"No?" Tina asked hopefully.

He shook his finger at her. "Never do that again."

Tina let out a tremendous sigh of relief. "Don't worry, Dad. I won't."

"I don't think it will do too much damage." Santa turned to George. "Sorry I grabbed that from you, son."

George beamed at the term.

"I always wanted a son," Santa muttered.

Clara frowned. "We have a son."

"You know, a real son. A son who wants to be here," he responded testily.

Clara shook her head. "Nick is our real son and you better be nice to him."

"Turn on the TV," Santa ordered.

Clara picked up the remote. "Where are your manners? What's the magic word?"

"Give me that thing."

She glared at him.

"Please," he groaned. She handed it to him and he plopped down on the couch. He aimed it at the TV and scanned the channels.

"Dad, I want you to know that we're ahead of schedule," Tina stated.

He raised his eyebrows. "Well, you hardly need us

then. We should go back home.”

Tina smiled. “I do need you, Dad. You and Mom have been an enormous help.”

“Then we’ll stay. I have to make sure you handle the sleigh properly. The foot pedals are a little tricky. The right one sticks.”

“I know. I had it serviced, and it doesn’t stick anymore.”

“Well, look at that, Clara. She knows everything,” he said, but Tina saw a twinkle in his eye.

“I’m learning,” Tina replied. “But I’m no expert like you.”

“You’re doing okay.”

That was high praise from her father.

“Oh, you just passed something.” Clara took the remote.

“...woman’s magazine claims Santa is real and, not only that, but that Santa is a woman.” The male anchor chuckled.

“Why not? Women do most of the work around here,” the female anchor retorted with a wry smile.

“Talk about a superwoman. Hope she can drive that sleigh straight,” he remarked.

“At least she won’t have to ask for directions,” she zinged back.

“So, she mentions elves and talking snowmen. Sounds like my night after a few cocktails,” he went on.

“I wish I had some elves helping around the house,” the female anchor quipped. “And we’ll be right back with the weather.”

“They made a joke out of it,” Tina said with disappointment.

“Most people aren’t ready to believe,” Clara said.

“This is good. No one will take it seriously,” Santa said.

“No, it’s not,” Tina argued. “I don’t want them to trivialize it. I want people to believe. I want people to have optimism and know that there’s good in the world.”

"Some people will believe," Clara assured her. "Just not everyone. Only the ones who are ready."

***

Tina sat down at her desk in front of her computer and opened up a new email. She considered for a moment before typing.

Hi Jill,
I liked the article. I thought it was moving and sincere. I'm not sure what I expected, but it was disillusioning when people didn't take it seriously and made it into a joke. Yet, surprisingly, we started receiving letters from adults. They don't ask for anything. They just thank us. I guess there are a few people out there who saw the truth and that touches my heart. I hope the article didn't affect your job negatively. I hope you had a nice Thanksgiving and have a Merry Christmas and a Happy New Year.
Thanks,
Santina

Tina read and responded to her other emails until a reply popped into her inbox.

Hi Santina,
I'm happy you liked the article. That was important to me. I expected to take some flak for it, but the joke is on them because we know the truth. My editor knew this would happen, but it was a good piece for the holiday issue and people liked it. We've gotten lots of letters about it, and it seems most people think it was just a cute holiday piece. That's fine with me. I did my job. It's nice to hear you've also gotten some positive letters. I hope you have a wonderful Christmas, although I know you'll be working. You have such a pure spirit, and I found it inspiring. Don't worry about my job. I'm excited about my

next project. I'll be off to Africa in a few months to do a story about building wells to provide access to clean water for impoverished communities. I hope the New Year is good to you. I believe in you!
Sincerely,
Jill

Tina smiled. There was nothing you could do about the naysayers, and that was okay. Perhaps she'd take a break from her computer and go downstairs to the mail room and read some letters. They always cheered her and reminded her about why she was there, why she'd disrupted her life and why her family had worked so hard and given up so much for generations. And would continue to do so.

It was about the kernel of joy that lives in each of us. That bit of us that wants to believe in the goodness of people and that the world will eventually gravitate towards harmony and peace. It pulls at us like a magnet. Children around the world were not so different. They craved love and happiness and weren't afraid to express it. And they didn't hesitate to believe in Santa. They were the true inspiration.

***

Tina appraised herself in the full-length mirror in the bedroom. She adjusted the red hat with the white faux fur trim. Her long hair hung down her back in a thick white braid. She encircled the wide black belt around her waist.

"Wow," George said. "You look the part."

She shrugged. "Just doing my job."

"Good luck." He drew her to him and kissed her. "I'm glad you don't have a beard like your father."

"Yes, but it'd keep my face warm." She rubbed her chin. "I'm so glad you're here."

"Me too. This whole place is unbelievable. I don't

think I'll ever get used to it." He gazed into her blue eyes. "I can't wait to see you fly off on the sleigh."

"I'm going to be totally wiped out when I get back. I'll probably just sleep for a few days," Tina warned. "Lisa and my parents will know how to take care of me."

"I'll be right here," he vowed. "I won't leave your side."

"Good." It was comforting to hear.

"I want you to know that this has been the best year of my life," George said with sincerity. "It's been an adventure ever since I met you, and now I'm married to the love of my life. I feel extremely lucky."

"Oh, George." Tina smiled at him with affection. "I'm the lucky one. This has been the best year of my life, too. I was so afraid you wouldn't want to deal with a long-distance relationship and I was going to lose you."

"Are you kidding me? I'd go to the ends of the earth for you, wife."

"What a coincidence." She giggled. "That's where I'm going tonight, husband."

George chuckled. "You continue to amaze me. I just can't wrap my head around it. How are you able to accomplish all that? How does it work?"

"It's the Gift. It was bestowed upon my family to allow us to do it," Tina answered. "I don't really understand how it works. I don't know if it speeds me up or slows down time or both."

"How does it feel?"

"It feels..." Tina furrowed her brow, trying to find the words. "It's exhilarating and I just feel... I don't know how to describe it. It feels like I'm filled with all this energy. It's like everything synchronizes perfectly and the air feels charged with magic. It shimmers and glimmers all around me."

"I don't know why Nick wouldn't be interested in doing this. How could you pass up an opportunity like this?" George shook his head.

"He has his own dreams. He's into his music."

"Lucky for me or I never would've met you."

"Lucky for me too," Tina said. "Besides, most of the year, it's hard work. He wouldn't have liked it. He needs a creative outlet. He would've been bored running the business."

"It doesn't seem boring to me."

"It's just like any other business most of the time."

"Not like any business I've ever seen. Most businesses don't have elves running around." He laughed and shook his head.

"I guess that's true." Tina smiled.

"I had a blast working here. I feel like a little kid when I'm here."

"Are you sure it's not because my parents are here?" she teased.

George grinned. "Your parents are great."

"Yes, they are." Tina gave one last look in the mirror. "And now it's showtime."

They stepped into the living room. Her black boots stood in the foyer and her gloves sat on the table by the door. Once she donned these items, she'd be ready to go.

"Oh." Clara clasped her hands together. "Look at our daughter, dear."

Santa came over and put his hands on both her shoulders. "Remember to let the reindeer lead the way."

"I will, Dad." Was that a tear glistening in the corner of his eye?

"Safe delivery," he said, giving her a quick hug.

"The suit looks great on her. You did a good job altering it," Clara told Walter.

"Thanks, Clara. I was happy to do it," Walter said.

"Let's move it along," Lisa urged. "The reindeer are waiting."

Everyone slipped on their coats and trundled downstairs. It was a tradition to exit through the back door from the large kitchen that was used to make gingerbread houses and other holiday treats. A sweet aroma permeated the warm room. Rows upon rows of gingerbread houses lined shelves along with jars of candy canes.

They filed outside into the chill of the night. Tina recalled watching her father climb into the huge sleigh weighed down with gifts. She and Nick had huddled with their mother in the cold until the red sleigh ascended into the sky and disappeared from view. Then they'd go inside for the soothing ritual of milk and cookies before bed.

When she was very young, it had upset her to see her father take off and fade into the dark sky. She feared he'd never come back. This was one of her earliest memories, but once she was old enough to understand that he'd return, it entranced her to see the sleigh rise up and sail away. She never tired of that magical moment.

The first year she'd nervously climbed into the sleigh, only Lisa and Walter had witnessed her departure. Now joining them were her husband and parents. She knew it was a sight to behold, but even more so, it was an indescribable experience. She could feel the magic swirling through the air and infusing her. It warmed and invigorated her.

Everyone embraced her in turn.

"We're so proud of you," Clara whispered in her ear.

"Good luck. See you soon." George kissed her. "I'll be waiting."

"You've got this," Walter assured her.

"You go, girl!" Lisa exclaimed, squeezing her tightly.

"Tina." Her father stood before her. "You've done a fine job. Yes, a fine job." He patted her shoulder.

"Thanks, Dad."

Tina stood, taking in the imposing figure of her father. She'd always been a little intimidated by him and a whole lot in awe. He was larger than life. They'd had their issues. She'd felt neglected while he'd attempted to prepare Nick to assume his role, but she understood the importance of this tradition. And it had certainly turned out differently than anyone had expected.

Blitzen snorted. The reindeer were impatiently jostling each other. She turned to them and took off her gloves to stroke each of them. Their fur was cold and coarse, and she could feel the great strength of their muscles poised to begin their long trek.

Tina took in a deep breath. The air sparkled and whirled around her, and the stars twinkled above. The moon was large and low, with a bluish tint. It seemed to beckon to her as the wind gusted and swept at her, longing to lift her. She turned to take a last look at everyone. They shivered in the icy gale. But she didn't feel the cold.

Tina grabbed onto the handles and climbed into the sleigh. She situated herself and tilted her face upward, her eyes taking in the velvet sky. Exhilaration washed through her and anticipation bubbled in her stomach. The Gift would carry her through this night. It would slow time itself for her.

Tina called to the reindeer to signal them. "Blitzen and Donner, Comet and Cupid, Dancer and Prancer, Dasher and Vixen and Rudolph. Dash away! Dash away!"

Tina held on as the sleigh budged with a shudder before easily gliding across the frozen ground. She watched the reindeer gallop and, suddenly, they lifted off the ground and sailed through the darkness. She was imbued with energy and elation. It all came down to this moment. All the hard work. All the stress and worry. All the obstacles. She'd made it through another tough year.

And now she had a wonderful husband. And Lisa was the best friend you could ever have. She had a family that was a little crazy, but lovable. It would still be difficult to endure the distance that separated her and George, but they'd find the time to be together. There would always be challenges ahead, yet she was so very happy. And she had the best father ever.

There was one last little detail as they swooped around one last time before they would disappear from sight. She knew what she must do. And it was so satisfying.

"Ho! Ho! Ho!" Tina's voice filled the night, and the wind carried it back to those on the ground. They jumped and cheered for her.

Yes. It had been the best year of her life. So far.

***

From the Author

I hope you enjoyed **Merrily Ever After!** Mrs. Claus is named after my mother Clara, who suggested the idea for the first book, **The Daughter Claus**. Finish this merry series by reading **The More the Merrier** for the heartwarming conclusion!

If you enjoyed this book, please post a rating or brief review on Amazon and/or Goodreads. I appreciate every one and it helps readers decide whether to read this book. Thank you!

Find out what happens next in **The More the Merrier!** The description and first chapter are on the following pages.

Each of my novels explores family and friendship, love and romance, and relationships and life. All are available on Amazon and free to read through Kindle Unlimited. Follow me on Amazon, BookBub, and Goodreads, where you can read my blog.

~*~*~*~*~*~*~*~*~*~*~*~

The More the Merrier (Book 4)

Does Santa want his job back?

Tina Claus is suffering from the stress of running the family business at the North Pole. It's taking a toll on her health and her long-distance relationship with George. To make matters worse, her mother is convinced that Santa is bored with retirement and wants his old job back. No way is Tina ready to give it up!

Meanwhile, Nick is still baffled by Isabella's flirtatious behavior as they face one last rock tour together and must get her to admit her feelings before they go their separate ways. And when a mysterious stranger is seen lurking around the toy shop, Lisa and Walter play detective to track down the intruder. But they have bigger problems! Gerta predicts a major storm that threatens the delivery on Christmas Eve!

Can Tina save her job and her relationship during this stormy time?

Christmas magic, girl power, and more merry fun are on the way! See how it all turns out in this final Santina Series story!

"Great finish!" Kayla Merta

"Fun, funny and romantic... It really doesn't have to be Christmas to enjoy this magical series of books." constant reader

"Wow! I really enjoyed these series... Thanks for such a wonderful read." Redhearts

Enjoy the first chapter next!

1 *Nut Job*

Santina Claus opened her eyes and stretched. What time was it? She glanced at the clock. Good. It wasn't too late. She was alone in bed and turned to look out the large window. It was another beautiful sunny day. A gentle breeze fluttered the lacy curtains, and she heard the faint sound of a guitar. It made her smile as she threw back the covers and jumped out of bed. But first, a trip to the bathroom.

George came in as she stood in front of the mirror braiding her long hair. He wrapped his arms around her from behind, and she looked at their reflection in the mirror. His long dark hair contrasted with her white hair. Together, they were striking. No wonder people stared at them.

"Hello, wife." He kissed her shoulder.

"Hello, husband." She turned to give him a kiss. "I should just let your sister braid my hair when she gets here since she likes to do it, and it's easier than braiding it myself."

"Are you sure you want to tell her, Tina?"

She sighed, releasing him, and he followed her back into the bedroom where they began making the bed.

"I don't know. I never thought this far ahead, but I don't see how we can keep it from her much longer."

"I know. Gemma is persistent. She's the one who asks questions and wants to visit us in the winter."

"But if we tell her, could she keep a secret? She won't tell your brother or your parents when she goes back to Boston, will she?" Tina stood holding a pillow.

"I think she can keep a secret, but I hate to put her in that position."

Tina sat on the bed. "I wish I could tell your grandmother. I love Grandma Grace."

"G.G. loves you too, and she'd sure get a kick out of it." He sat beside her. "So would my mother. You know how much she loves Christmas."

"Yes." She sighed again. "I always thought I'd marry somebody from the North Pole. I never imagined I'd have to hide who I am from my in-laws."

"You thought you'd marry Kai," George said.

She shrugged. "There were other boys I dated, but I always thought..." She bit her lip. "When I came to Florida to go to college, I never intended to go back. I wanted to get away from my childhood and have my own life. I never thought I'd end up back home running the toy shop while the man I love is in Florida." She put her hand on his face. "I married the right guy and I'm so lucky."

"I'm the lucky one." He kissed her lightly. "I'm sorry you couldn't have the wedding you wanted."

"Oh, our wedding was perfect, George." Tina smiled. "You'll see what a Winter White wedding is like when we go to Kai and Sonia's wedding. It's funny. Everybody here wants a June wedding, but up there everyone wants a November wedding."

"Is your brother going?"

"I'm sure Nick will go. We grew up with Kai, but he won't be able to bring Isabella because she doesn't know who we are."

"I wonder how serious it is between them."

"Who knows what's going on with them? First, it was about publicity and now who knows?"

"I still can't believe my father-in-law is Santa Claus." George shook his head. "And I can't figure out what to call him. I mean, I can't call him Santa or Mr. Claus out in public, and I don't want to call him Nick because that's your brother's name."

"You should probably just call him Grumpy." Tina giggled and put her hand to her mouth.

"At least I can just call your mother Clara."

"Do you think your mother read that article in *Modern Woman's World* magazine about me a few months ago?" Tina asked.

"I don't think she reads a lot of magazines."

"I guess it's lucky that most people took it as a joke. I don't know why I ever did that interview. What was I thinking?" Tina shook her head at herself. "I'd better get dressed. Your sister will be here soon."

"And then there's the matter of giving our parents grandchildren." He grinned and pulled her to him. "We've been married almost a year. We should at least make the effort."

Tina squirmed away from him. "Not so fast. We don't even live in the same place half the time. How could we raise a family?"

"We'll figure it out."

"That's way in the future. Anyway, I'll be heading back up north soon and you'll be going out on tour." Tina opened the closet.

George groaned. "It seems like we're either rehearsing, touring, or in the studio recording."

"That's called success, silly husband."

"I'm not complaining. I just hate being apart."

"Me too." She held up a sundress. "What do you think?"

"Everything looks good on you."

"I'm serious."

"So am I."

"I never got to wear stuff like this at the North Pole. I love pastel colors." Tina looked at him. "Are you going to change?"

George looked down at his shorts and *Black Ice* T-shirt.

"What for? It's just my sister."

***

"I wish I had hair like yours," Gemma said as she braided Tina's hair. "Mine is too thick and curly. I just have to let it do what it wants."

"I wish I had hair like yours," Tina responded. "Mine is too straight."

"But it's so silky. I just love the feel of it and the white color is amazing. Nobody has hair this color except your brother and older people."

"I think it makes me look pale," Tina confessed.

"Not at all. It makes you look… delicate."

"Do you like the scones?" George asked.

"You know I love your scones." Gemma popped a piece into her mouth. "I have no talent for baking or cooking like my brothers. Isn't that funny?" she said to Tina.

"Are you seeing Loren later?" Tina asked.

"After band rehearsal." Gemma turned to her brother. "What time do you think you guys will finish?"

"I don't know. We're having a band meeting first," George answered. "It depends on whether Nick and Loren start debating about something."

"I thought they were getting along now," Tina said.

"Well, they're not fighting over Isabella anymore, but they still seem to disagree a lot."

"Do you think Loren still likes her?" Gemma asked casually.

"He only flirted with her to annoy Nick," Tina assured her. "He's totally into you."

"I don't like playing games," Gemma said.

"I've never seen him like this before and I've known him a long time," George said.

"Good." Gemma smiled and finished braiding Tina's hair. "All done." She broke off another piece of her scone. "So when is *Black Ice* going back out on tour? Loren wasn't sure."

"We're waiting to hear from our manager, Robin, about that. He'll be at the meeting, so we might find out tonight."

He gave Tina a surreptitious look, and she shook her head slightly.

"Do you want something to drink?" he asked Gemma.

"Just some water."

"We'll be right back." He took Tina's hand and pulled her into the kitchen. "Don't you want to tell her?" he asked in a hushed tone.

"I want to tell her. I really do. It's just going to open up a bunch of questions and she'll be thinking about it all night and she'll have to keep it from Loren," Tina reasoned. "Maybe we should wait until tomorrow."

"Let's just tell her. I trust her. She won't tell him if we ask her not to."

"I don't want to put her in that position..."

Gemma entered the kitchen. "What's going on? What aren't you telling me?"

"I... Are you working on a new book yet?" Tina deflected her attention.

Suddenly Gemma beamed. "Oh, my God! You're pregnant! I swear I won't tell anybody. When are you due?"

Tina blushed and quickly shook her head. "No. I just... I really want to know about your new book."

"Bummer."

Gemma turned and headed back into the living room. She sat cross-legged on the brown fabric couch.

"I'm not sure what I want to work on next. I want to write something a little different, you know?"

"Uh huh." Tina sat on the couch, relieved that the subject had changed.

"Do you guys want a smoothie? We have a mango and a pineapple," George offered.

"Sounds good." Tina nodded.

"Mom told me about something interesting she read," Gemma continued. "It sounds pretty crazy, but it might make a good book."

"What is it?" Tina asked, picking at a scone.

"I think I could take the basic idea and make it into something good," Gemma mused. "You won't believe it, though."

"What?" Tina smiled.

"It was an article in a magazine about a woman who

believes she's Santa's daughter." Gemma laughed.

George froze on his way to the kitchen. He turned back slowly.

"I guess it was on the news too, and the reporter who wrote it said it was true, but, of course, it was a joke." Gemma shook her head. "The woman was obviously a nut job, but it might make a good story if I can figure out an angle. What do you think?"

"I don't think she's a nut job," Tina responded hesitantly. "How do we know what's true and what's not? Just because we don't know about something doesn't mean it's not true."

"Tina," George said. "Just tell her."

"Tell me what? Why are you guys acting so weird?" Gemma demanded. "You're not telling me something."

Tina cleared her throat. "It's awful that people don't believe anymore. Children believe. Your little nephew, Evan, believes. But there's so much cynicism. It just makes me so sad…"

George sat on the ottoman and took her hand. He looked at Gemma.

"I didn't believe it at first either. I had to see it with my own eyes, but I've been there and it's all true."

"What are you talking about?" Gemma looked from one to the other.

"You can't tell anybody," Tina stressed. "Not your family. Not Loren. Obviously, George and Nick know, but you see what happens when it gets out. People either think we're crazy or they stalk us. I shouldn't have done that interview." She shook her head. "I thought with all the bad news in the world that people needed something good…"

"You guys are totally messing with me," Gemma accused.

"No, we're not," George claimed. "This is going to blow your mind. Tina is…"

"It's me," Tina said. "I'm the nut job."

***

May your life be filled with great books!

Made in the USA
Monee, IL
12 July 2026